# How to Play
# Good Opening Moves

## Edmar Mednis
### International Grandmaster

### Revised by Burt Hochberg

**Random House**
**Puzzles & Games**

**Library of Congress Cataloging-in-Publication data is available.**

0 9 8 7 6 5 4 3 2 1
May 2002

ISBN: 0-8129-3474-1

New York   Toronto   London   Sydney   Auckland

# Contents

| | |
|---|---|
| *Reviser's Note* | vi |
| *Preface* | vii |
| | |
| **Chapter 1: What Is the Opening?** | 1 |
| Section 1: General Considerations | 1 |
| 2: Specific Principles | 4 |
| | |
| **Chapter 2: Quality of White Opening Moves** | 9 |
| Section1: Perfect Moves | 9 |
| 2: Mediocre Moves | 11 |
| 3: Poor Moves | 13 |
| | |
| **Chapter 3: Quality of Black Opening Moves** | 14 |
| Section 1: Perfect Moves | 14 |
| 2: Mediocre Moves | 22 |
| 3: Poor Moves | 24 |
| | |
| **Chapter 4: Evaluation of Moves: The Practical Approach** | 25 |
| | |
| **Chapter 5: Sicilian Defense: Basic Principles** | 50 |
| Section 1: Introduction | 50 |
| 2: Basic Principles | 52 |

**Chapter 6: Sicilian Defense: Advanced Play**     65

**Chapter 7: Queen's Gambit Declined: Basic Principles**     78

**Chapter 8: Queen's Gambit Declined: Advanced Play**     87

**Chapter 9: Bad Moves: How Not to Play Them**     96

**Chapter 10: Castling: Early or Late?**     114

**Chapter 11: Pawn Play: Center, Formations, Weaknesses**     124

*To my sisters, Aiga and Inita*

# Reviser's Note

This new edition differs from the previous edition (1982) in the following ways:

- The chess moves have been converted from English descriptive notation to English algebraic notation.
- Diagrams have been added to make the moves and variations easier to follow without a chessboard.
- The layout of the moves has been expanded to aid comprehension.
- A few minor corrections have been made to the text.

May 2002                                                    Burt Hochberg

# *Preface*

There is no shortage of books published on the chess openings. The reasons are clear: the opening is a very important part of the game, and a tremendous amount of technical material is readily available. By their very nature these books are encyclopedic and are concerned with a single opening or various groups of openings. Since opening theory is expanding very rapidly, such books invariably contain material that has become obsolete even before the books themselves have been published. Nevertheless, they are indispensable for the professional master, both for reference purposes and as a starting point for his or her independent studies. The best series of such books is the five-volume *Encyclopedia of Chess Openings.*

But what of the chess player who enjoys chess and wants to improve his or her competitive success, but has neither the time nor inclination to memorize hundreds of variations? What he or she really needs is guidance on how to obtain good positions in the opening without relying on reams of memorized analysis. This book is aimed at exactly this type of player and uses the techniques that I have developed in many years of successful group and private teaching. The emphasis throughout is on principles. Starting with the very first move, the reader learns how to select good opening moves just by observing the three primary principles of good opening play.

Since the book's approach is an original one, most of the research material is original also. The rest has been obtained from what can be considered the standard sources: personal contacts, leading chess periodicals, books. When appropriate, credit is given in the text. As with all of my previous books, my partner here too has been my wonderful blonde wife Baiba. My deepest gratitude goes to her for typing the entire manuscript and for continuous moral support.

The following list contains the standard meanings of the symbols used throughout the text:

! = a strong move
!! = a very strong move; a fantastic move
? = a bad move; a weak move
?? = a horrible move; a blunder
!? = an enterprising move; a move worthy of consideration
?! = a dubious move, for theoretical or practical reasons

Since this book is about principles rather than analysis, technical chess errors should be at a minimum. Still, given the complexity and inexhaustability of chess, some errors are almost inevitable. The author accepts responsibility for all of these. Your assistance in bringing them to my attention will be appreciated.

New York, 1982                                             Edmar Mednis

# CHAPTER 1

# *What Is the Opening?*

## SECTION 1. General Considerations

The beginning phase of a game of chess is called the opening. What is the relative importance of the opening as compared to the middlegame and endgame?

The question can be argued from various points of view, yet there is no definitive answer—the complete chess player should aim to be equally adept at all these phases. Nevertheless, a valid case can be made that the study of openings should be the first area undertaken. The Germans have an expression that goes something like: "A good opening means that the game is half won." Such a saying should not be taken too literally, but its point is well taken. Gaining an advantage early is not only of obvious practical value but is also significant psychologically. Knowing that you stand well should give you confidence during the action to come; conversely, your opponent, realizing that he stands badly, may not be able to pull himself together to face the ensuing middlegame. Thus, an opening advantage can well lead to an easy win in the middlegame.

What have some of the leading players in chess history expected to get out of the opening? J. R. Capablanca considered the main principle to be "rapid and efficient development," with the corollary that when the pieces are brought out, they must be "put in the right places." He also gives some excellent advice about what to do when confronted with an unfamiliar move—as happens many times to everyone! "Play what you might call the common-sense move." By this he means following the general principle stated above. Even if the move played may not turn out to be the very best one (usually subsequent analysis is required to discover this), the plan of aiming to bring out the pieces quickly to safe locations will in the large majority of cases produce a perfectly good move.

Larry Evans provides a modern technical definition when he says "The opening is a fight for space, time and force." Svetozar Gligoric emphasizes the factor of time; that is, the rate at which the chess pieces enter the fight. According to him, "The efficient use of time in the opening requires generally that each move should be used to develop a new piece." Lajos Portisch presents a more philosophical outlook, painting with a broad brush, as it were: "Your only task in the opening is to reach a playable middlegame." Anatoly Karpov's games show that he is in basic agreement with Portisch's thesis. Robert J. Fischer's approach to the opening is a very demanding one: if possible, he prefers to sweep his opponent off the board at the very start.

Of course, the specific goals for White and Black are different. Success in the opening for White means that he emerges with at least a slight pull. Black, on the other hand, can feel completely satisfied if he has equalized. Both Fischer and Karpov have been very successful in retaining at least some of White's natural advantage. Playing Black against them has always been a most disagreeable task. Karpov's goal with Black has changed considerably since he became world champion in 1975. Formerly, when playing against world class grandmasters, he was satisfied to eventually obtain safe, sound equality and a draw. But as world champion he was interested in winning every game, and therefore his openings with Black became considerably more dynamic.

For Fischer, dynamic positions have invariably been the rule. That's why his main weapons for Black have always been the Najdorf Sicilian against 1 e4 and the King's Indian and Grünfeld against 1 d4. These opening systems require exceedingly accurate play by White, lest the initiative pass to Black. Fischer enjoyed such situations and was always ready to seize whatever chance was offered. Nevertheless, his primary concern was to play sound chess, doing whatever the position requires. If White's play was perfect, he realized that it would take some time before he could equalize. There was seldom any unjustified outburst of activity in his games. As Robert Byrne tells it, they had a session of analysis together in the late 1960s during which Fischer, in looking over some of Byrne's games, expressed surprise whenever he noticed that Byrne was jumping the gun in playing for the attack with the Black pieces.

Disapprovingly, Fischer advised: "You've got to equalize first with Black before looking for something."

In general, it is safe to say that White should aim for at least some advantage out of the opening, whereas Black should strive for equality. Depending on whether Black's primary goal is to win or to draw, his aim should be either dynamic or safe equality. Does this mean that no other move may be played except that which official theory currently considers the best? Of course not—other moves or plans are often valid for either psychological or practical reasons. For instance, the anticipated effect of some surprising move on an opponent who is known to feel uncomfortable when taken out of theory may be of great practical value. Or a player may know, understand, and enjoy playing a line which theoreticians regard as slightly inferior. No matter. Every player is well advised to play whatever opening he likes and understands best.

It is also important to keep a certain logical perspective on one's approach. It is simply foolhardy for White *voluntarily* to choose a line that—if Black plays correctly—hands the initiative over to the opponent. Experimentation by White should be limited to those moves where the ultimate result is no worse than equality. Black for his part shouldn't risk a line where—if White plays correctly—Black will wind up so far behind the eight ball that his chances for recovery are slight. Experimentation by Black should be limited to moves that give White only a slight advantage, with at most an additional marginal inferiority for Black as compared to the theoretically best lines.

How long is the opening? The dividing line between the end of the opening and the start of the middlegame is not a sharp one. Many current books on openings present analysis often running into move 20 and beyond. It should be clear that in such cases the game has already entered the middle stage. A simple yardstick is that when the initial piece development has been accomplished, we are ready for the middlegame. Normally this occurs within the first 10–15 moves. Alternatively, we can consider the opening over when at least one of the players has accomplished most of the specific objectives of opening play. These objectives or goals are discussed in the next section.

The ultimate key to successful play is understanding chess.

Though a fair amount of specific knowledge is required in the opening, it is still of considerably greater value to understand how to play good opening moves, rather than to have memorized lots of complicated variations. Capablanca, as he himself readily admitted, was not an expert in formal opening theory. In 1919 a match was arranged in Havana between him and the Serbian master Kostic, who was noted for his great opening memorization. As Capablanca described him then: "Kostic knows by heart every game played by a master in the last twenty years, and a considerable number of games of much older date." Nevertheless, Capablanca was not in the least daunted, and, with his much deeper chess understanding, swept the first five games. His great opening knowledge notwithstanding, Kostic thereupon resigned the match.

# SECTION 2. Specific Principles

As a science progresses from its infancy to widespread acceptance, tenets that seemed at first to be grounded in witchcraft are replaced by those based on logic and verified by experimentation. This is the stage that chess has reached today. The basic principles are agreed to and understood by the leading scientists (top players). It can be stated with a high degree of confidence that the basic principles of opening play will not be superseded by new discoveries in the foreseeable future. These principles have obtained a kind of universality. Thus, the principles described in this book will remain valid for at least the next one hundred years.

This does not mean, however, that the age of discovery is over. If anything, just the opposite is true. Many new opening schemes are still to be discovered, and our understanding of many current openings increased. As more is learned about certain currently unpopular or unsatisfactory systems, some of them may well be rehabilitated. The direction of discovery should be generally positive. I expect that many new good plans will be established. There is no reason to think that any current lines that are based on both sound logic and practical successes will suddenly be proven unsound. Therefore, the tools presented in this book for learning how to find good opening moves will remain valid. Good moves will remain good; the progress of opening theory will lead to the discovery of more good moves.

The three areas of greatest significance for opening play are king safety, piece development and center control. The importance of the king is not a controversial matter, and the need for its safety in the middlegame is well recognized. It is important, too, to keep the king's safety in mind from the very first move. It is false security to think that one's king must be safe just because the opponent doesn't have many pieces out. The counterpoint here is that the potential defenders of the king are also not yet mobilized. A sudden end can befall even the White king. Two grotesque examples: A) 1 f4 e6 2 g4?? Qh4 mate; B) 1 d4 Nf6 2 Nd2?! e5!? 3 dxe5 Ng4 4 h3?? Ne3!!, and White, in this game between two French masters, resigned, since the "necessary" 5 fxe3 allows 5 ... Qe4+ 6 g3 Qxg3 mate.

The logic of rapid and purposeful development has been referred to earlier and at this point needs no further discussion.

The value and importance of the center is not, however, sufficiently appreciated by a majority of chess amateurs. The center and the control thereof are of utmost significance in both the opening and the middlegame. If we consider such popular sports as basketball, ice hockey, football or soccer, we see that most of the action is concentrated in the center of the field. Local skirmishes may take place in the corners, ends or sides, but the grand plays generally begin at or near the center. A similar situation exists in chess. The exact center in chess consists of the squares d4, e4, d5, e5 (shown within the solid lines in Diagram 1). These are the four squares of maximum importance and are called the *primary* central squares. Also of considerable importance are the squares adjoining these primary squares, called the *secondary* central squares. These form the larger square c3–c6–f6–f3, as shown by the dotted lines in Diagram 1.

Viewed strictly from the standpoint of central importance, the secondary central squares along the c-file are equivalent to those along the f-file. Therefore, it would seem to be just as logical to use the respective f-pawns for central action and support as to use the c-pawns for this purpose. Yet when we recall the need for king safety we see that this is not so, since moving the f-pawn of necessity loosens the king position. This is always a factor with the king still uncastled and may be significant even when the king has castled kingside. This of course does not mean that the use of the f-pawn for central purposes is taboo, but whenever such use is contemplated one must feel sure that the advantage to be gained

### DIAGRAM 1

**BLACK**

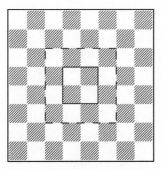

**WHITE**

*Primary and secondary
central squares*

in the center is not outweighed by the decreased safety of the king.

No such constraints exist for the use of the c-pawn, unless queen-side castling is anticipated. It also follows from the above discussion that weaknesses of squares on the f-file in the vicinity of one's own king are potentially more dangerous than similar weaknesses on the queenside; i.e., vulnerability at f2, f3 and f4 is more serious than at c2, c3, c4. In general: the c-pawn is a natural instrument for central action, but before employing the f-pawn for this purpose, make sure that the king remains safe.

The importance of controlling the center has been known to those following chess theory ever since Wilhelm Steinitz started to expound on strategic principles in the late 19th century. At that time control of center was synonymous with actual possession. For example, to control d4, it was thought White must either have a protected pawn or piece there. It was the hypermodern school of the 1920s that significantly deepened our understanding of central play. What mattered, according to the hypermodernists, was not possession but control, and it may be even advantageous to achieve this from long range! 

In synthesizing the ultimate truths of the classic teachers and the hypermoderns, we have indeed learned that the center and its control are of major importance. What our free thinking has taught us is that how we accomplish this is usually irrelevant. If we again consider the d4 square in Diagram 2, any and all of the following methods for controlling it are of equivalent value:

**DIAGRAM 2**

**BLACK**

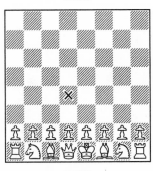

**WHITE**

*Control of the d4 square*

A) 1 d4
B)  1 e3
C)  1 Nf3
D) 1 b3 followed by 2 Bb2
E)  1 c3

For realizing the advantage of the first move, White can do better than alternatives B) and E). However, for the purpose of controlling d4 all are valid. As a particular opening is played and the need develops to control d4, any one of them can be considered with a clear chess conscience.

With the above background in mind it is now possible to formulate the following three principles of correct opening play:

1. Bring your king to safety by castling.
2. Develop your pieces toward the center so that they are ready for middlegame action.

3. Control the center either by actual possession or by short-range or long-range action of pieces or pawns.

The specific quality of various opening moves will be considered in the next two chapters. One overriding standard must be emphasized: unless an opening move works towards at least one of the above objectives, it is not a good move.

# CHAPTER 2

# *Quality of White Opening Moves*

## SECTION 1. Perfect Moves

Why not the best?

According to current chess understanding, five of White's possible first moves are absolutely perfect, and there is no valid reason for not choosing one of them to start the game. Although these moves are of equivalent quality, the nature of possible play arising from them can be quite varied, so all kinds of individual styles can be accommodated by these "perfect five." From ultrasharp to safe and stodgy—choose your move and system, and attain the most promising position possible within your chosen field!

These perfect moves are shown by the arrows in Diagram 3. Listed in order of most to least active, they are:

### DIAGRAM 3

BLACK

WHITE

*The five perfect first moves
for White*

### 1 e4

The most active move. White puts a pawn on the important e4 square, thereby also exerting pressure on d5. Diagonals are opened for the queen and king bishop and rapid deployment of the latter becomes possible. Development of the king knight and king bishop allows for rapid kingside castling. Generally open and active play is the characteristic of openings resulting from 1 e4. This move is useful towards achieving all three opening objectives.

### 1 d4

This can be considered the queenside counterpart of 1 e4. White puts a pawn on the important d4 square, thereby also exerting pressure on e5. A diagonal is opened for the queen bishop and part of a file for the queen. Immediate play arising from 1 d4 is usually concerned with the center and queenside. The move serves two of the opening objectives. Active strategic play is the major characteristic of openings resulting from 1 d4.

### 1 c4 (English Opening)

On the face of it this may not seem to be of major usefulness since it furthers only the queen's development. Its principal value comes from the pressure it exerts on d5, to be reinforced by the logical follow-up 2 Nc3. Then the queen knight is able to exert maximum central pressure, while the c-pawn has been already mobilized for this purpose. When taking into account the continuation 2 Nc3, it can be seen that 1 c4 serves to further two of the opening objectives. Play in the English Opening usually develops on the queenside, with the queen often making use of the a4, b3 and c2 squares. The English is a fairly active strategic opening.

### 1 Nf3

This move is ideal from the standpoint of opening principles, as it furthers all three objectives. Unless he later chooses to transpose into some other opening, White will continue with 2 g3, 3 Bg2 and 4 0–0. In just four moves White will then have castled, exerted actual central pressure with the king knight and latent pressure with the king bishop. Admittedly, this is not an aggressive plan, yet it is fully in accordance with modern opening principles. Often games started with 1 Nf3 transpose into other lines: following up with 2 d4 leads to d-pawn openings, while the continuation 2 c4 can lead to the English.

### 1 g3

Though this appears passive, it also helps to achieve all three opening objectives. After 2 Bg2 (the development of a bishop on the flank is called a fianchetto) the bishop controls the important e4 and d5 central squares. As a follow-up, White can pay further attention to the d5 square by playing 3 c4 and 4 Nc3, or he can complete kingside development with 3 Nf3 and 4 0–0. As can be seen, 1 g3 is a very flexible move and—though not active—is nevertheless perfect.

There is a sixth first move that is almost perfect and is just a shade below the previous five in value. This is 1 b3, the queenside counterpart of 1 g3. After 2 Bb2 White will have sound pressure against the key d4 and e5 squares. In the late 1960s and early 1970s, Bent Larsen was very successful with 1 b3, and it is deservedly named after him. However, extensive theoretical work has shown that 1 b3 is somewhat inferior to 1 g3 for the following two reasons:

1.  It does not further the safety of the king by preparing kingside castling. (Queenside castling is not attractive in this opening.)
2.  Additional pressure on e5 is difficult to achieve, since f4 would lead to some weakening of the king position.

# SECTION 2. Mediocre Moves

If a person doesn't want to play the best, then at the very least he should choose one of the three second-best possibilities. Each of them does have positive features, but because of inherent deficiencies, the highest rating that can be given them is "mediocre." These are shown in Diagram 4.

**DIAGRAM 4**

BLACK

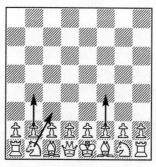

WHITE

*The three mediocre first
moves for White*

### 1 b4

With the plan of 2 Bb2, aiming at the d4 and e5 squares. In addition, the pawn controls the secondary central c5 square. It is unprotected, however, and after such normal responses as 1 ... e6 or 1 ... e5 White will soon have to take time out for a3. Note that the same central purposes are served equally well by 1 b3, and with *no* disadvantages.

### 1 Nc3

The queen knight is placed on its best central square. But by precluding the use of the c-pawn for central purposes, White makes it more difficult to establish a fully harmonious central/piece–development combination. It is just too early to say on move one "I won't use the c-pawn."

### 1 f4

This move contributes nothing to development and slightly weakens the kingside. Its redeeming feature is that it serves to exert pressure on the central e5 square.

# SECTION 3. Poor Moves

All other opening moves are poor. Don't play them! A brief comment about each of them is all that is necessary:

1 a3, 1 a4—these moves waste time.

1 Na3, 1 Nh3—both develop knights *away* from the center.

1 h3, 1 h4—these waste time *and* weaken the kingside.

1 f3—this does nothing for development and weakens the kingside.

1 g4—seriously weakens the kingside.

1 c3, 1 e3, 1 d3—unnecessarily passive. These are reasonable moves for Black but make no sense for White. White should play as White, not as Black!

Since I don't want you to play these moves, I haven't shown them on any diagram!

# CHAPTER 3

# *Quality of Black Opening Moves*

In general we can say that what is good for White is also good for Black, and what is poor for White is even worse for Black. For instance, all of White's five perfect first moves are so good that Black can in each case respond symmetrically! On the other hand, the move 1 ... g5 is akin to suicide. Of course, White's first move can inhibit certain responses and reduce the value of others.

The following sections will show how Black should and should not play. In all cases, I assume that White has opened only with perfect moves. If White has done otherwise, Black should play the same good moves. What will happen is that Black will get an excellent position in less time!

## SECTION 1. Perfect Moves

Perfect moves are those that help further at least one of our stated opening objectives while having no strategic or tactical deficiencies. Just as in Chapter 2, we shall discuss them in order, dealing first with the replies to White's most active moves.

### A) 1 e4

Black has the following seven perfect responses, as shown in Diagram 5:

## DIAGRAM 5

**BLACK**

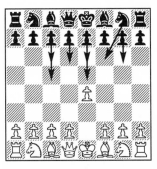

**WHITE**

*Black's seven perfect replies
to 1 e4*

### 1 ... c6

Though incidentally freeing a diagonal for the queen, the primary purpose of 1 ... c6 is to establish control of the d5 square. Black plans 2 ... d5, so that after, e.g., 2 d4 d5 3 exd5 cxd5! his central control is equal to White's. So 1 ... c6 is not only centrally motivated but also prepares a challenge to White's active e-pawn. This safe and sound opening, called the Caro-Kann Defense, is popular with careful strategists. Former world champion Tigran Petrosian was a steady practitioner, and another champion, Anatoly Karpov, selected it for his 1974 match with Spassky.

### 1 ... c5

Black immediately exerts pressure on d4 and is ready to intensify this with Nc6. This is the world–famous Sicilian Defense, once Robert J. Fischer's exclusive defense to 1 e4 and currently Black's most popular response to that opening move. We will take a close look at this important opening in Chapters 5 and 6.

### 1 ... d6

Black protects the e5 square and opens his queen bishop's diagonal. Usually this move is followed by 2 ... Nf6 and 3 ... g6, and is then called the Pirc Defense. Until the middle 1940's this was thought to be inferior, but now it is recognized as a fully satisfactory opening.

**1 ... e6**

This can be looked on as analogous to 1 ... d6. Black plans to challenge e4 by 2 ... d5, thereby also establishing firm control of his d5 square and exerting pressure on e4. The diagonals of the king bishop and queen are also opened. This is the well-known French Defense. Former world champion Mikhail Botvinnik was an early adherent of it. The German grandmaster Wolfgang Uhlmann plays it exclusively, and grandmasters Viktor Korchnoi and Lajos Portisch have it in their repertoires.

**1 ... e5**

This is just as good as White's first move: it controls e5 and attacks d4, while opening the diagonals for the queen and king bishop. However, since the pawn is unprotected here, Black will have to endure some pressure on it. Further play is required to determine what opening will result.

**1 ... Nf6**

Strategically logical, as the king knight is developed to its preferred square while it attacks White's e-pawn. Of course, White can chase the knight away with 2 e5 and gain some further time by attacking it again. This defense was originated by world champion Alexander Alekhine in the early days of the hypermodern 1920s and is therefore named after him. It took some time for its tactical soundness to be established. It conclusively established its theoretical soundness when Fischer twice chose it in his 1972 match with Spassky.

**1 ... g6**

Black will develop his king bishop toward the center with 2 ... Bg7, while at the same time preparing rapid kingside castling. Since White is given the opportunity to build up a strong center, Black's plan was long thought to be somewhat dubious. Latest analysis shows that Black can cope with White's initial central superiority, and therefore 1 ... g6 must be rated as perfectly good.

However, Black must understand the nuances of this defense very well, as otherwise White's center will smother him. Some writers call this opening the Modern Defense, but, since such a name will seem ludicrous some years hence, the generic King's Bishop Fianchetto or the historical Robatsch, after the Austrian grandmaster Karl Robatsch, seems more appropriate to me.

### B) 1 d4

Black also has seven perfect replies here, as shown in Diagram 6:

**DIAGRAM 6**

BLACK

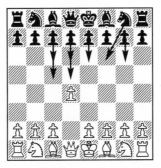

WHITE

*Black's seven perfect replies
to 1 d4*

### 1 ... c6

Preparing to continue with the centrally desirable 2 ... d5. After 2 c4 d5 Black has selected the Slav Defense of the Queen's Gambit Declined, whereas after 2 e4 d5 we have reached, by transposition, the Caro-Kann Defense. Though rarely played, 1 ... c6, when followed by 2 ... d5, is a truly perfect move.

### 1 ... c5

Black immediately challenges White's d-pawn. After the normal response 2 d5, Black has the choice of playing 2 ... e5 to set up the old Benoni formation, or to challenge White's advanced d-pawn with a later ... e6, which leads to the Modern Benoni. In either case, White retains a clear space advantage. Very accurate defense by Black is necessary, but with it his prospects are satisfactory.

**1 ... d6**

This exerts control on e5 and frees the queen bishop. After 2 c4 Nf6, King's Indian formations result, and after 2 e4 Nf6, play usually proceeds on Pirc lines (see above). The immediate 1 ... d6 is unusual, yet fully in accordance with opening principles.

**1 ... d5**

With exactly the same point as White's excellent move: controlling d5, attacking e4, opening the queen bishop's diagonal and preparing the development of the queen.

**1 ... e6**

This move controls d5 and frees both the queen and king bishop for action. After 2 e4 Black will enter the French Defense with 2 ... d5, whereas after 2 c4 Black has the choice of bringing about the Queen's Gambit Declined with 2 ... d5 or continuing his kingside development with 2 ... Nf6.

**1 ... Nf6**

Black's most flexible reply and currently the most popular move in tournament play. By developing the king knight toward the center, Black furthers every one of his opening objectives.

**1 ... g6**

With the same ideas as after 1 e4 g6: to fianchetto the king bishop and prepare for kingside castling. After 2 d4 Bg7, play develops according to the closed d-pawn openings, while 2 e4 Bg7 leads to the more open play characteristic of e-pawn openings.

**C) 1 c4**

Again Black has seven perfect replies as shown in Diagram 7:

**DIAGRAM 7**

BLACK

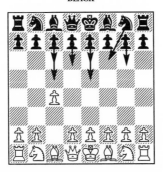

WHITE

*Black's seven perfect replies
to 1 c4*

**1 ... c6**

Black plans to challenge White's c-pawn and establish control of d5 by means of the coming 2 ... d5. After 2 d4 d5, the Slav Defense results, and 2 e4 d5 leads to a less usual variation of the Caro-Kann.

**1 ... c5**

Again aping White's logical plan: Black exerts pressure on the centrally important d4 square, he is now ready to develop the queen knight without disadvantage to its ideal c6 square and the queen is also made available for queenside play.

**1 ... d6**

Guarding e5 and freeing the queen bishop. Black can follow up with 2 ... e5, 2 ... Nf6 or 2 ... g6, depending on his own wishes. Though not common, 1 ... d6 is fine in all respects.

**1 ... e6**

Guarding d5 and freeing the queen and king bishop. Black will continue with either 2 ... d5 or 2 ... Nf6.

**1 ... e5**

An active plan whereby Black occupies a key central square, attacks d4 and frees his queen and king bishop.

**1 ... Nf6**

Again the most flexible response, furthering all opening objectives. Black can choose a large number of systems on his second move: 2 ... c6, 2 ... c5, 2 ... e6 and 2 ... g6.

**1 ... g6**

Black immediately shows that he wants to fianchetto his king bishop. This is a very flexible plan, and since 1 c4 is not a primary central move, Black doesn't have to worry about White building up an unduly strong center.

**D) 1 Nf3**

As shown in Diagram 8, Black has the following seven perfect moves:

**DIAGRAM 8**

BLACK

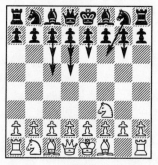

WHITE

*Black's seven perfect replies*
*to 1 Nf3*

A) **1 ... c6**
B) **1 ... c5**
C) **1 ... d6**

D)  **1 ... d5**
E)  **1 ... e6**
F)  **1 ... Nf6**
G)  **1 ... g6**

These moves have appeared before, and here bestow the same advantages and are justified by the same rationale. Since 1 Nf3 is not an active thrust, Black has no practical need to prepare ... d5 by the preliminary 1 ... c6. However, there is nothing wrong with 1 ... c6, and often the same position is reached as after 1 ... d5. For instance, the popular Reti Opening can start 1 Nf3 d5 2 c4 c6, or alternatively 1 Nf3 c6 2 c4 d5.

### E) 1 g3

Since this is White's least active move, every one of Black's eight possible good moves is feasible. As shown in Diagram 9, they are:

**DIAGRAM 9**

BLACK

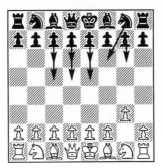

WHITE

*Black's eight perfect replies to*
*1 g3*

A)  **1 ... c6**
B)  **1 ... c5**
C)  **1 ... d6**
D)  **1 ... d5**
E)  **1 ... e6**

F)  **1 ... e5**
G)  **1 ... Nf6**
H)  **1 ... g6**

Each of these moves has been discussed earlier in depth, and the same reasoning applies here as well. Since the reader has been studying the individual sections, I am sure that he has noticed well before now how the good replies are repeated. What is good against one opening is also good against a different one, because the same *principles* of opening play apply. The eight perfect Black moves, according to opening principles, are the ones shown above. Unless there is a clear specific reason why it is not playable, you cannot go wrong in choosing one of them no matter what White's first move is.

There is another first move by Black that deserves special mention. In the late 1970s British masters, led by grandmasters Anthony Miles and Raymond Keene started playing 1 ... g6 with generally good success. The idea behind this move is similar to the one behind 1 .. g6, in that the fianchettoed bishop will bear down on two primary central squares—in the case of 1 ... b6 these are d5 and e4. But 1 ... b6, in comparison with 1 ... g6, has the disadvantage of doing nothing for king safety by means of castling (castling queenside is generally inappropriate in these lines). The lack of castling means both that Black's king may remain less secure and that Black's counterplay in the center cannot be supported by his king rook. A partial compensation for Black is that his fianchettoed queen bishop can naturally bear down on White's e-pawn in case White plays for a strong center with an early e4.

It is still too early to give a definitive answer regarding the objective value of defenses starting with 1 ... b6. Chess theory, with its endless search for truth, will give its answer in due course. My best guess is that 1 ... b6 is a bit too passive to be objectively rated as perfect. It is in any case no more than a shade worse than the perfect moves. Perhaps, after the less active 1 Nf3, there are no theoretical deficiencies at all in the reply 1 ... b6.

# SECTION 2. Mediocre Moves

With so many perfect moves available for Black, why choose any other? I don't really know, yet there are players who think that they can do better by taking the opponent "out of the book." Moves that have certain positive features and can therefore qualify as "mediocre" are as follows:

**A) 1 e4**

**1 ... Nc6.** The queen knight is developed to its preferred square, but this occurs too early. After 2 d4 White gets a significant central superiority, no matter whether Black continues with Aron Nimzovich's 2 ... d5 or the alternative 2 ... e54.

**1 ... d5.** Challenging White's e-pawn is surely logical, but Black's problem is that after 2 exd5 Qxd5 3 Nc3 Qa5 4 d4, he has lost time with his queen, and the position of White's d-pawn on the fourth rank gives him a clear central superiority. This is, however, a recognized opening, It is called the Center Counter Defense in English–speaking countries and the Scandinavian Defense in other parts of the world.

**B) 1 d4**

**1 ... Nc6.** By playing the queen knight out too early, Black has central difficulties after 2 c4, 2 e4 or 2 d5.

**1 ... f5.** The Dutch Defense. Black exerts some control over e4 and dreams of attacking chances later on against White's kingside. The drawbacks of this move are obvious: development is not furthered and the kingside is weakened. Unless one is a grandmaster, it is extremely easy to land in a strategically hopeless situation on the Black side of the Dutch.

**C) 1 c4**

Again the two mediocre moves are 1 ... Nc6 and 1 ... f5, and the discussion in part B applies equally well here.

**D) 1 Nf3**

The best that can still be said about 1 ... Nc6 and 1 ... f5 is that they are mediocre. Black's queen knight's development could work well if White continues quietly, but if White plays the active 2 d4!, then Black's voluntary obstruction of his c-pawn again makes it impossible to establish a fully satisfactory central formation.

**E) 1 g3**

1 ... f5 again neglects development and weakens the kingside. Against 1 ... Nc6 White should seize his chance for central superiority with 2 d4!. Then the best that Black can achieve are some strategically unsatisfactory variations in the Chigorin Defense.

Again the reader has no doubt noted how certain patterns of mediocrity are repeated. Against closed openings these are the premature development of the queen knight (although admittedly to its best square) and the centrally helpful yet non-developmental 1 ... f5. Against 1 e4, apart from the queen knight's move, Black can also choose the overly aggressive 1 ... d5.

# SECTION 3. Poor Moves

Moves that were poor for White will be even worse for Black. Therefore, never play 1 ... a6, 1 ... a5, 1 ... Na6, 1 ... f6, 1 ... g5, 1 ... h6, 1 ... h5 or 1 ... Nh6. Their White counterparts were poor, and each of them is a bit more than Black can afford.

Two moves do deserve some explanation of why they should be rated as poor rather than mediocre. The first is 1 ... b5 as a counter to 1 d4, 1 Nf3 or 1 g3. As the reader will recall, White's 1 b4 was rated as mediocre. Black, being a move behind, can not afford both to weaken his queenside and to lose the time necessary to defend the unprotected pawn. For instance, after 1 d4 b5 2 e4 Bb7 3 f3, Black has to lose a move to protect his b-pawn.

The other "unplayable" move worth special mention is 1 ... d5 as a response to 1 c4. There are two reasons why 1 ... d5 is worse against 1 c4 than against 1 e4:

1. After 2 cxd5, White has exchanged a secondary central pawn (the c-pawn) for Black's primary central pawn, so White will be able to build up a considerably stronger center than against the Center Counter Defense. White will have both a d-pawn and an e-pawn, whereas Black's only remaining primary central pawn will be the e-pawn.

2. After the normal moves 2 cxd5 Qxd5 3 Nc3, White will have an edge in development and also the stronger center after 4 d4. And because the position remains relatively closed, Black's opportunities for counterplay are considerably less than in the Center Counter Defense.

# CHAPTER 4

# Evaluation of Moves: The Practical Approach

On the first move everything is rather clear. If you play in accordance with opening principles, your choice will be fine. But what about move two or move 10? As play develops, the position becomes more complicated, and, necessarily, more specific thinking is required when selecting your move. It cannot be overemphasized that, on balance, your choices will work out much better if they are in accordance with the basic principles. To give preference voluntarily to a move that does not contribute to development, is irrelevant to center play or is deleterious to king safety is madness unless it also offers some fantastic positive feature(s).

In fact, such features exist only rarely. Most moves that are unmindful of opening principles turn out to be clearly inferior. Yet the yen for experimentation often grips chess masters as well as amateurs. Too often we think that perhaps "in this specific position" we can choose a move that violates basic principles, because a special situation exists. Statistics show that such special situations exist much more rarely than we—in our creative optimism—think.

What kind of benchmarks should we use in deciding whether a move is good? By far the best guide is its conformity to good opening principles. It should further at least one of our basic objectives. The kind of thinking to use will be demonstrated in the following examples, illustrating both traditional and new ideas. All the major openings will be considered, with the exception of the Sicilian Defense and the Queen's Gambit; these will be covered in depth in Chapters 5–8.

Dubna 1979

*RUY LOPEZ*
White: Georgiev Black: Razuvaev

**1 e4 e5**

**2 Nf3**

Developing the king knight toward the center with a gain of time is a perfect move and White's best choice here.

**2 ... Nc6**

The e-pawn needs protection, and providing it by developing the queen knight to its best central location is Black's most popular response. Since Black has selected the e-pawn to be his main central bastion, the use of his c-pawn for central work is neither required nor readily possible. Therefore, there is no disadvantage in the queen knight's blocking the c-pawn in this case.

**3 Bb5**

Completing the development of the minor pieces on the kingside and preparing to castle immediately. By attacking the queen knight, White exerts indirect pressure on Black's e-pawn. Thus the bishop move can actually be seen as part of White's plan to achieve central superiority. White's third move has brought about the well-known Ruy Lopez opening.

**3 ... a6**

Chasing back the bishop, since White can't win a pawn by 4 Bxc6 dxc6! 5 Nxe5?! because of 5 ... Qd4, and Black regains the pawn with a fine game. It is not at all obvious that 3 ... a6 is a good move, however, and it required extensive tests in master games before the value of the move was established.

**4 Ba4**

Maintaining the status quo. An alternate plan of equivalent value is 4 Bxc6 dxc6 5 0–0!.

**4 ... Nf6**

Developing the king knight to its best central square.

**5 0–0**

And so in five moves White has achieved good central pressure and development while bringing his king to safety by castling. White has no need to fear 5 ... Nxe4 since after 6 d4! he will win back the pawn by force. Though not completely obvious, this conclusion can be anticipated because the open nature of the position will require Black to concern himself with the safety of his own king, and will have to castle rapidly. White will be able to capture Black's e-pawn while the latter is catching up in development.

**5 ... b5**

A controversial move. To prevent threats to his e-pawn, Black protects his queen knight from attack by White's bishop, but this move chases it onto the diagonal aiming at f7. Unless Black can castle quickly, this square can become very vulnerable. The time-tested, most common move is the quiet development with 5 ... Be7.

**6 Bb3 Be7**

**7 Re1**

### DIAGRAM 10

**BLACK**

**WHITE**

*Georgiev-Razuvaev,*
*after 7 Re1*

By protecting the e-pawn with his rook, White brings about the normal position in the Closed Ruy Lopez, which usually results after 5 ... Be7 6 Re1 b5 7 Bb3. Instead, White can force Black to solve more difficult problems with the aggressive 7 d4!, since after 7 ... exd4 8 e5 is very annoying.

Note that after 7 Re1 White's rook is centrally placed. At the moment, its primary function is defensive, but it can also readily become aggressive along the e-file.

**7 ... 0–0**

Black's King is now safe.

**8 c3**

Planning to build a strong center with 9 d4.

**8 ... d6**

Protecting the e-pawn and opening up the diagonal of the queen bishop. If White proceeds with the immediate 9 d4, Black can exert strong pressure on the d-pawn with 9 ... Bg4.

**9 h3!**

The sole purpose of this move is to be able to play d4 without allowing the pin ... Bg4. Since Black cannot prevent the coming d4 and has no immediate threat, White can afford this loss of time. The position after White's 9th move has been analyzed to great depth, since Black has many possibilities. Formerly the Chigorin Variation (9 ... Na5 10 Bc2 c5) was very common, and in the 1970s Breyer's idea of 9 ... Nb8 10 d4 Nbd7 caught fire.

**9 ... Bb7!?**

Only in the last couple of years has this move appeared in master practice. Why has it taken so long for this discovery to be made? Based on basic opening principles, the move is surely worth very serious investigation. Black completes the development of his minor pieces and positions the queen bishop so that it bears directly on the center. Whenever Black's queen knight moves away, the bishop will be attacking White's e-pawn.

**10 d4 Re8**

The basic position in this sub-variation. Black's rook is posted both to support his e-pawn and indirectly to attack White's e-pawn. Since White has some central superiority, he still has the slight advantage that comes with his right to make the first move. His most consistent plan now is to start developing the queenside

### DIAGRAM 11

BLACK

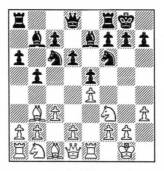

WHITE

*Georgiev-Razuvaev,*
*after 9 … Bb7!?*

pieces with 11 Nbd2. Instead, White shows in this game that he is satisfied to draw against his better–known opponent. The Soviet grandmaster playing Black is not satisfied with such a result, but by continuing the game with second-rate moves, he avoids the draw only to lose instead: 11 Ng5 Rf8 12 Nf3 h6?! 13 Nbd2 exd4?! 14 cxd4 Nb4 15 Qe2 c5 16 a3 Nc6 17 dxc5 dxc5 18 e5 Nh7 19 Ne4 c4 20 Bc2 Re8?! 21 Bf4! Nf1 22 Qe3 Ng6 23 e6! Nxf4 24 exf7+ Kxe7 25 Qxf4+ Kg8 26 Qf5! Rf8 27 Qe6+ Rf7 28 Rad1 Qc8 29 Qg6 Rxf3 30 Nd6! Bxd6 31 Rxd6 Kf8 32 gxf3 Qc7 33 Rde6 Qf7 34 Qxf7+ Kxf7 35 Bg6+ Black resigns.

Hastings 1978/79

*ALEKHINE'S DEFENSE*
White: Speelman Black: Suba

**1 e4 Nf6**

**2 e5**

The pawn, challenged by the knight, must return the challenge, since letting the king knight remain on its present post allows Black easy development.

## 2 ... Nd5

## 3 Nf3

Developing the king knight can't be bad. Even so, the central 3 d4 at least equally good, and considerably more flexible. Then after 3 ... d6 White can choose, for instance, the very sharp Four Pawns Attack with 4 c4 Nb6 5 f4, or the sound, strategic 4 Nf3.

## 3 ... d6

Opening lines for development while at the same time challenging White's outpost is the only logical plan.

## 4 Bc4

A reasonable spot for the bishop, but it's really too soon to tell whether it is the *best* one. The normal, flexible 4 d4! is better suited to retaining an advantage.

## 4 ... c6

Keeping the knight in the center without blocking off the queen bishop's diagonal, as would occur in case of 4 ... e6.

## 5 Nc3?!

Developing the queen knight to its best square runs the risk of incurring doubled pawns. Since nothing is gained in return, the plan is dubious. Again, White's best is the simple 5 d4.

## 5 ... Nxc3

## 6 bxc3

Capturing this way enhances White's central pawn prospects. The opposite would be true after capturing away from the center with 6 dxc3?!.

## 6 ... d5!

A strategically logical change of plans by Black. White was willing to accept doubled pawns in the hope that the superior development of his minor pieces would yield full compensation. Therefore, Black chooses to close the position so that he can complete his development without allowing White to undertake anything

**DIAGRAM 12**

BLACK

WHITE

*Speelman-Suba, after 6 bxc3*

immediate. Once Black's development is complete, he can start to exploit White's structural weakness—the doubled c-pawns.

**7 Be2 Bg4!**

Black needs to play ... e6 to develop the king bishop, but doing so on move seven would lock in the queen bishop. So Black develops it first.

**8 Rb1 Qc7**

**9 d4 e6**

**10 0–0 Nd7**

**11 h3 Bxf3**

Since Black's pawn formation does not harmonize well with his light-squared bishop, and since the position is rather blocked, Black is fully justified in this exchange. But 11 ... Ba5 is also all right.

**12 Bxf3 0–0–0**

Black's king is safe, his position has no structural weaknesses and he can develop the king bishop at his leisure. White has no compensation for his immobile c-pawns. On the whole, Black's prospects are slightly better. In further play Black obtained a

### DIAGRAM 13

BLACK

WHITE

*Speelman-Suba,
after 12 ... 0-0-0*

winning position, but his error on move 33 allowed White to salvage a draw: 13 Qd3 Nb6! 14 Be2 Kb8 15 Bg5 Rc8 16 Rb3 h6 17 Bh4? c5! 18 dxc5 Nd7 19 Rb2 Nxc5 20 Qd4 g5 21 Bg3 Ne4 22 Rfb1 Nxg3! 23 Ba6 b6 24 Rxb6+ axb6 25 Rxb6+ Kh8 26 Bb5 Qa7! 27 Ra6 Bc5 28 Rxa7+ Bxa7 29 Qa4 Rc7 30 Bc6+ Kb8 31 Qb5+ Kc8 32 Qa6+ Kd8 33 Bxd5! Re8? (The winning method is 33 ... exd5! 34 Qf6+ Kd7 35 Qxh8 Ne4 36 Qf8 Bxf2+ 37 Kf1 Ke6, as given by Suba) 34 Bc6 Ne2+ 35 Kf1 Nxc3 36 Qd3+ Nd5 37 c4! Rxc6 38 cxd5 Rb1+ 39 Ke2 exd5 40 Qxd5+ Kc8 41 Qa8+ Bb8 42 Qa6+ Kd7 43 Qd3+! Kc7 44 Qd6+ Draw.

Helsinki 1979

*FRENCH DEFENSE*
White: Sznapik Black: Hort

**1 e4 e6**

**2 d4 d5**

The basic position in the French Defense. White's e-pawn is challenged and it must either move or be protected. It is easy to see that 3 exd5 exd5! allows complete symmetry and equality.

### 3 Nd2

The best way of protecting the pawn is with the queen knight. For this purpose, 3 Nc3 looks ideal, but after that move Black can apply an annoying pin with 3 ... Bb4. Therefore, currently the text move—originally championed by the great German player Siegbert Tarrasch—is very popular. White prevents the potential pin and keeps the c-pawn free for central action. There also are two negative aspects, however: the diagonal of the queen bishop is now blocked, and the knight exerts less pressure on the center (that is, on the important d5 square).

### 3 ... Nf6

Developing the king knight with a gain of time by attacking the e-pawn is a good, logical plan. Theoretically playable, though strategically somewhat inconsistent, is to give up the fight for the center immediately by playing 3 ... dxe4. After 4 Nxe4 White's d-pawn controls more central space than Black's e-pawn, while Black's queen bishop remains blocked. A perfectly good alternative, though, is 3 ... c5, whereby Black tries to take advantage of the less active location of White's queen knight by posing a direct challenge to both of White's central pawns.

### 4 e5

Still harmless is 4 exd5 exd5. Since there is no fully satisfactory way of keeping the e-pawn protected, White advances it with a gain of time.

### 4 ... Nfd7

The best response. Instead, 4 ... Ng8 is a clear loss of time, whereas 4 ... Ne4 risks having a vulnerable doubled pawn after 5 Nxe4.

### 5 c3

Since Black will be attacking the d-pawn—the base of White's central pawn chain—by means of an imminent ... c5, White reinforces it. Of equivalent value are the developmental 5 Bd3 or 5 f4, supporting the e-pawn.

### 5 ... c5

Note how the dynamics of Black's counterplay against the White center alter as the situation warrants. First he applies pressure to White's e-pawn, and then, when that pawn is stabilized, Black switches over to attack the d-pawn.

### 6 Bd3

It must be logical to place the bishop on a diagonal where it both helps to influence the center and aims at Black's kingside. A strong alternative is 6 f4. At the cost of one tempo he might otherwise spend developing his pieces, 6 f4 reinforces control of the key e5 square and prepared in certain situations to advance against Black's kingside with f5.

### 6 ... b6

Since the central pawn formation of the French allows White's light-colored Bishop much more scope than the corresponding Black bishop, Black prepares to exchange his bishop after the coming ... Ba6. This idea is based on sound strategic principles. Its disadvantage is that it costs considerable time in a position where White already has a nice space advantage. The most usual move for Black is the consistent, developmental 6 ... Nc6, bringing the queen knight to its ideal square while attacking the d-pawn.

### 7 Ne2

There is no smooth way of preventing Black's planned ... Ba6, so White does best to complete the development of his minor pieces. Then, if White so chooses, he can castle early.

But where should the king knight go? Developing it to e2 allows it to head for f4 or g3. White can follow this with a queen move (most probably Qg4) directed against Black's kingside. Additionally, the f-pawn can be used in the coming play. Thus the text move is quite good. Attractive, but less effective, is 7 Ngf3, since White will then have great difficulties in formulating an attack against Black's kingside, and in the French Defense the kingside is where White's prospects most often lie.

According to the latest theory, however, White's strongest move is the "anticentral" 7 Nh3!. Of course, this is an exception to the principle that the pieces should be developed toward the center. The specific strengths of the move are:

## DIAGRAM 14

BLACK

WHITE

*Sznapik-Hort after 7 Ne2*

1.  The knight can get to both f4 and g5—the two most useful attacking locations for the knight.
2.  The diagonal d1–h5 remains open for White's queen, and it can therefore easily reach the attacking squares g4 or h5.
3.  The king knight is developed so that White can castle immediately.
4.  After castling, f4 becomes quite feasible, with the plan of attacking Black's kingside by means of an eventual f5.

**7 ... Ba6**

**8 Bb1?!**

That White does not want to exchange his good Bishop is understandable, but this retreat both costs time and hands over a nice diagonal to Black's bishop. Correct is 8 Bxa6 Nxa6 9 0–0, and White's spatial advantage plus his edge in development gives him the better chances.

**8 ... Nc6**

Developing while at the same time threatening to win the d-pawn.

**9 Nf3 b5?**

The sortie with the b-pawn costs two tempos while accomplishing nothing positive. Correct is either the developmental 9 ... Be7 or 9 ... cxd4, opening the queenside. In either case, Black has approximate equality.

**10 0–0 b4**

**11 Re1!**

### DIAGRAM 15

BLACK

WHITE

*Sznapik-Hort,*
*after 11 Re1!*

White has castled, substantially completed his development, and retained his clear central superiority. Black has no coherent way of coping with White's spatial and developmental advantages. Although he is a world class player, Black is now decisively defeated: 11 ... Bxe2 12 Qxe2 cxd4 13 cxd4 Qb6 14 Be3 Be7 15 Bd3 Rc8 16 Rac1 Rc7 17 h4! h5 18 Bb5! g6 19 Bxc6 Rxc6 20 Rxc6 Qxc6 21 Rc1 Qb7 22 Bg5! Bxg5 23 Nxg5 Ke7 24 Qf3 Rf8 25 Qf4 f5 26 Qd2! Rb8 27 Nh3! Nc8 28 Rc5 Nd7 29 Rc2 Nf8 30 Kh2 Ke8 31 Qc1 Kd7 32 Qh6 Ke8 33 Nf4 Qf7 34 Nd3! Qe7 35 g3 b3 36 axb3 Kf7 37 Nf4 Kg8 38 Nxg6 Qg7 39 Qxg7+ Kxg7 40 Nf4! Rxb3 and Black resigned without wait for White's reply.

South Africa 1979

*QUEEN'S INDIAN DEFENSE*
White: Unzicker Black: Korchnoi

**1 d4 Nf6**

**2 c4**

By far the most active central move. The c-pawn bears on the important d5 square and the queen knight can be developed at White's leisure to its ideal location at c3. In addition, the queen can now be developed toward the queenside.

**2 ... e6**

Acting on the key d5 square and allowing the development of the king bishop. After that is accomplished, Black will be able to castle.

**3 Nf3**

One of the two best and most popular moves. The king knight is developed to its ideal central square and the way is prepared for kingside castling.

The alternative is 3 Nc3, which is thought to be a bit sharper since it "threatens" the strong central advance 4 e4. Many players currently do not play 3 Nc3 because they prefer not to allow 3 ... Bb4, pinning the knight and establishing the Nimzo-Indian Defense.

**3 ... b6**

This is the move characteristic of the Queen's Indian Defense. Black will fianchetto his queen bishop, thereby exert strong pressure on d5 and particularly e4. But Black also has three other logical plans: (A) 3 ... d5, transposing into the Queen's Gambit Declined (see Chapter 7); (B) 3 ... c5, challenging the d-pawn and, after 4 d5 exd5 5 cxd5 d6, reaching the Modern Benoni Defense, and (C) 3 ... Bb4+, offering to trade off the bishop (after 4 Bd2) and achieve rapid castling.

**4 g3**

White fianchettos his king bishop to oppose Black's on the central diagonal. This is by far the most popular move. Also good and in accordance with opening principles are 4 Nc3 and 4 e3.

### 4 ... Ba6!?

But what is this? Has Black lost his senses? Wasn't the point of 3 ... b6 to continue 4 ... Bb7? The answer is yes: 4 ... Bb7 is in fact the normal response and leads to the main line of the Queen's Indian.

Nevertheless, the eccentric–looking text move has an important point, and therefore has shown itself to be a satisfactory alternative to 4 ... Bb7. From the a3 square the bishop attacks the c-pawn, and White's most efficient response is 5 e3. But coming on the heels of 4 g3, 5 e3? would lead to a noticeable weakening of the light squares on the kingside, since White could no longer fianchetto the king bishop while it is needed to protect the c-pawn. As will be seen shortly, all other methods of protecting this pawn also have sufficient shortcomings to allow Black good chances for ultimate equality.

### 5 Qa4

Protecting the c-pawn while applying pressure against Black's queenside. This is White's most usual move. However, the queen is somewhat exposed here and no longer exerts much influence on the center. But there is nothing better. After either 5 Qc2 or 5 Nbd2, Black effectively challenges White's d-pawn with 5 ... c5!, since the response 6 d5 is now impossible. After 5 b3, Black gets good counterplay with 5 ... Bb4+! 6 Bd2 Be7! 7 Bg2 c6! 8 0–0 d5.

### 5 ... Ne4?!

A new and interesting idea, but too eccentric to be fully satisfactory. Black tries to exploit the awkward position of White's queen, but moving an already developed piece twice more loses far too much time. After the indicated 5 ... c5 or 5 ... c6 Black's prospects for equality are bright.

### 6 Bg2 Nd6

### 7 c5!

Active play is required to take advantage of White's momentary edge in development. Harmless is 7 Nfd2?! c6 8 Qc2 Nf5 9 Nf3 d5

### DIAGRAM 16

**BLACK**

**WHITE**

*Unzicker-Korchnoi,*
*after 5 ... Ne4?!*

10 cxd5 cxd5 with Black at least equal in Trois–Tarjan, Riga Interzonal 1979.

**7 ... bxc5**

7 ... Nb7 8 b4 gives White a powerful bind on the queenside.

**8 dxc5 Nb7**

**9 c6!**

At the cost of a doubled pawn, White destroys Black's counterplay and completes his own development efficiently. Since White
will exert pressure along the c-file against Black's pawns, he has
every expectation of at least recovering his investment.

**9 ... dxc6**

**10 Nc3! Bd6**

**11 0–0 0–0**

**12 Rd1**

### DIAGRAM 17

BLACK

WHITE

*Unzicker-Korchnoi,*
*after 12 Rd1*

Note how consistently all of White's pieces have been developed toward the center. Black's pieces, on the other hand, particularly his knights, stand awkwardly rather than usefully. White's advantage, though not large, is both pleasant and free of risk. The game continued: 12 ... Qe8 13 Nd4 Nd8 14 Be3 Bb7 15 Nb3 Nd7 16 Ne4 Nb6 17 Qa5 f5, and now, instead of 18 Nec5?, which led to nothing after 18 ... Bc8 (White still won when Black, in an equal position, overstepped the time limit on move 56), Unzicker suggested the straightforward 18 Nxd6 cxd6 19 Bxb6 axb6 20 Qxb6 Qe7 21 Na5 Ra6 22 Qb4 c5 23 Qb5. The more active position, absence of weaknesses and potential benefit from the passed a-pawn—all mean that White's opening advantage has been carried through into the middlegame. Note also how effortlessly White recovered the pawn sacrificed on move nine.

Amsterdam 1978

*ENGLISH OPENING*
White: Timman Black: Romanishin

**1 c4 e5**

**2 Nc3 Nf6**

**3 Nf3 Nc6**

The play so far is clear and sound by both sides: each has pawn presence in the center and has developed the knights to their ideal squares.

**4 e3**

With the idea of establishing a strong center with 5 d4 by enabling the e-pawn to recapture on d4. Black should either strive for complications while developing the king bishop with 4 ... Bb4 or select the modest developing move 4 ... Be7, a plan which Karpov has used successfully.

**4 ... Qe7?!**

### DIAGRAM 18

BLACK

WHITE

*Timman-Romanishin,*
*after 4 ... Qe7?!*

A novelty. By pinning White's e-pawn, Black prevents it from recapturing on d4. However, the cost in time, the anti-developmental consequence of the queen's blockade of the king bishop and the fact that the queen is not well placed on e7—all this suggests that Black's plan can hardly succeed.

**5 d4! exd4**

**6 Nxd4**

Even though White has had to capture with the king knight, the consequences of the respective fourth moves are clear: White is ahead in development and has superiority in the center, while the position of the black queen makes it difficult for Black to complete his kingside development.

**6 ... g6?!**

It is logical for Black to want to fianchetto the king bishop, but this move allows a nasty attack on the c-pawn. Therefore, 6 ... d6 first was correct.

**7 Ndb5!**

Usually in such closed openings, the prospects for successful cavalry charges so early in the game are slight. Yet the clumsy location of Black's queen and White's edge in development change the normal odds.

**7 ... d6**

**8 Nd5! Nxd5**

**9 cxd5 Ne5**

**10 f4!**

White now has an undisputed central superiority. With his 11th move he extends his existing edge in development by a further gain of time.

**10 ... Ng4**

**11 Be2 Nf6**

**12 Qa4!**

White's spatial advantage and superior development, coupled with the black king's inability to castle, puts Black in a most unpleasant situation. If now 12 ... Bd7, 13 Qc4! leaves Black in a quandary, and 12 ... c6 13 dxc6 bxc6 14 Nd4 Bd7 15 Nxc6 gives White a pawn and the superior position. Black therefore chooses an endgame where his "only" disadvantage is a missing pawn: 12 ... Kd8 13 Nxa7! (with the threat 14 Nc6+) 13 ... Qe4!? 14 Qxe5 Nxe5 15

## DIAGRAM 19

**BLACK**

**WHITE**

*Timman-Romanishin,
after 12 Qa4!*

Nxc8 Kxc8 16 Bd3 Nc5 17 Bc2 Bg7 18 a3 Re8 19 Ke2 Na4 20 Rb1 Nb6 21 Rd1 Ra5 22 Bb3 f5 23 Bd2 Ra8. Black has no compensation for the pawn, of course, and White won on move 75.

São Paulo 1979

*RETI OPENING*
White: Stean Black: Ljubojevic

**1 Nf3 Nf6**

**2 g3**

White plans to complete his kingside development and only then look for an active plan.

**2 ... b5!?**

Black also wants to contest the light-squared central diagonal and thus prepares to fianchetto the queen bishop. He thrusts the b-pawn two squares forward in order to control the c4 square. The pawn is somewhat weak here, but because White, with 2 g3, has effectively relinquished his option to attack it with his king bishop (the bishop now belongs on g2 rather than on the f1-a6 diagonal), Black can just get away with his aggressiveness.

**3 Bg2 Bb7**

**4 0–0**

In just four moves White has brought his King to safety, developed his king knight and king bishop toward the center and prepared for concrete action.

**4 ... c5**

Grabbing more space in the center and on the queenside.

**5 d3**

White's first central pawn move, controlling the primary e4 and secondary c4 squares and allowing development of the queen bishop.

**5 ... Nc6**

Continuing the development of his queenside forces. Black so far has been able to neglect his kingside development because White is not aiming for any kind of direct attack against his king.

**6 e4**

The first active central move. White is now ready to continue with e5, and so Black prevents it in the most normal manner.

**6 ... d6**

**7 Nc3**

Developing the queen knight with a gain of time. Advancing the b-pawn further is no particular gain for Black, since White will then be able to start undermining it.

**7 ... b4**

**8 Nd5! Nd7!**

Black needs to chase White's queen knight back with a gain of time. Inferior are both 8 ... Nxd5 9 exd5, with a development and spatial advantage for White, and 8 ... e6?! 9 Nxf6+ Qxf6 10 c3!, with White again ahead in development and Black's queen clumsily placed.

**DIAGRAM 20**

BLACK

WHITE

*Stean-Ljubojevic,*
*after 8 ... Nd7!*

**9 c3 e6**

**10 Nf4**

Stean considers 10 Ne3! more accurate in view of the forthcoming play in the center.

**10 ... bxc3**

**11 bxc3 Nce5!**

**12 d4**

This position is slightly in White's favor. He is better developed and has more central space. Black has no fundamental weaknesses, however, and with the coming exchange of a pair of knights, his defensive burden is decreased. Black's play must be accurate to hold on, and in the game he achieved ultimate equality as follows: 12 ... Nxf3+ 13 Bxf3 Be7 14 Rb1 Rb8 15 d5 e5 16 Ng2 Ba6 17 Rxb8 Qxb8 18 Be2 Bxe2 19 Qxe2 0–0 20 Ne3 g6 21 Qa6 f5! 22 Qd3 fxe4! 23 Qxe4 Nf6 24 Qa4 Draw.

## DIAGRAM 21

**BLACK**

**WHITE**

*Stean-Ljubojevic, after 12 d4*

Lone Pine 1979

*KB FIANCHETTO OPENING*
White: Seirawan Black: Miles

**1 g3 e5**

An active, perfectly good response.

**2 c4**

After the immediate 2 Bg2, Black could occupy the center with 2 ... d5. Therefore White establishes a direct pawn presence himself and only later will continue with the planned development of the kingside.

**2 ... c6**

A very demanding approach. Black is determined to enforce ... d5. He already has good central presence, thanks to his e-pawn, but is determined to have a lot more. This is a very double-edged plan, because White—with the advantage of the first move—will be able to start undermining Black's imposing-looking center very quickly.

**3 Bg2 d5**

**4 cxd5 cxd5**

**5 e4!**

White establishes his own strong central presence while challenging Black's e-pawn. Clearly unsatisfactory now is 5 ... exd4?! because after 6 Nf3 White will effortlessly recapture the pawn and Black's isolated d-pawn will remain a chronic weakness.

**5 ... d4**

**6 f3!**

### DIAGRAM 22

**BLACK**

**WHITE**

*Seirawan-Miles, after 6 f3!*

Again challenging the e-pawn. Throughout, White gives a classic demonstration of how to cope with and undermine prematurely advanced center pawns. If now 6 ... exf3?!, then 7 Nxf3, and White's king knight has landed on its ideal square with a gain of time while Black's isolated d-pawn will remain weak.

**6 ... f5**

The bastion in the center must be held. Yet there are also disadvantages to this natural move: Black's kingside is weakened as are the dark squares (in particular e5), and the queen bishop's scope is decreased.

**7 Nh3!**

Remember that White's immediate strategic plan is to complete the development of his kingside. The only square available for the king knight is h3, and it is not a bad one in this case because the knight will be able to go on to f4.

**7 ... Nc6**

Normal and good.

**8 0–0 Be7**

**9 Nc3**

Developing the queen knight to its ideal square, where it will be able to pressure Black's d-pawn.

**9 ... Nf6**

**10 Bg5!**

Completing the development of the minor pieces and indirectly applying pressure on the d-pawn. If now 10 ... 0–0?!, then 11 Nf4!, and Black's d-pawn is in mortal danger. He must therefore bring up his queen bishop to help defend his center.

**10 ... Be6**

**11 Nf4**

Developing the temporarily wayward king knight toward the center with a gain of time.

**11 ... Bf7**

**12 e3**

White's d-pawn also needs support, and this is the simplest and best way of providing it.

**12 ... 0–0**

And so Black has brought his king to safety by castling, the minor pieces are developed and his central influence seems secure. Nevertheless, White's next move points up the weakness in Black's camp:

**13 fxe4!**

### DIAGRAM 23

**BLACK**

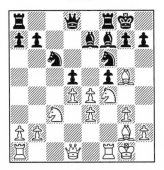

**WHITE**

*Seirawan-Miles,*
*after 13 fxe4!*

Black's problem is that he has no good way of recapturing *in order to retain his central influence.* As a matter of fact, the lesser evil here is 13...Nxe4! 14 Bxe7 Nxe7, though White's more active position and the weaknesses of Black's d-pawn and dark squares give White a steady plus. Inferior is 13 ... fxe4?! because of 14 Bh3! Qd6 15 Nb5 Qd8 16 Ne6 Bxe6 17 Bxe6+ Kh8 18 Bf4 Ne8 19 Qh5 a6 20 Nc3 Nf6 21 Qh3, and White's forces apply very strong pressure on Black's position.

Also inferior is the game's 13 ... dxe4?! because it not only yields White an immediate passed protected d-pawn but, even more important, Black's center pawns remain vulnerable to a further successful undermining. White realized his advantages in the following exemplary fashion: 14 Bh3 g6 15 g4! fxg4 16 Bxf6! gxh3 17 Bxe7 Qxe7 18 Qg4 Bc4 19 Rf2 Rf5 20 Nxh3 Rh5 21 Rg2! Rh4 22 Qg3 Rf8 23 Ng5 Rh5 24 b3! Bd3 25 Nd5 Qd7 26 Nf4 Rh6 27 Rd1 Rf5 28 h4 Nxd4 (desperation in a lost position) 29 exd4 Qxd4+ 30 Kh2 Qe5 31 Ngh3 Qf6 32 h5 Bb5 33 Rgd2 g5 34 Rd5! Rxd5 35 Rxd5 Qb2+ 36 Ng2 Rxh5 37 Rxb5 Black resigns.

# CHAPTER 5

# *Sicilian Defense: Basic Principles*

## SECTION 1. Introduction

Of all of Black's responses to 1 e4, by far the most popular in master chess is 1 ... c5, the Sicilian Defense. Its popularity is based on both fundamental and psychological factors. The Sicilian was Robert J. Fischer's primary (and almost exclusive) weapon against the e-pawn from the time he excited the chess world by winning the 1957/58 U.S. Championship at the age of 14 up to the 1972 world championship match against Boris Spassky.

The chess world admired Fischer's successes and great fighting spirit. Since the Sicilian Defense was so intimately associated with Bobby, his admirers felt that there must be something good and, indeed, almost magical about it. Many of the young, upcoming masters started playing it, and in due course this led to significant new discoveries in the theory of this defense, which in turn further enhanced its reputation and therefore its popularity. Currently, at least half of the games starting with 1 e4 turn out to be Sicilians.

Let us look again at the basic starting point, shown in Diagram 24.

The reasons for playing the Sicilian and the strategic ideas behind it are:

1. Black's 1 ... c5 is so dissimilar to White's 1 e4 that, invariably, very unbalanced positions result. In competitive chess this greatly increases Black's practical winning chances. When a master needs to win with Black, his natural opening choice is the Sicilian. In the later stages of his 1972 match with Fischer, when he was far behind and needed to win, Spassky turned exclusively to the Sicilian even though it was not a primary part of his opening repertoire.

2. Black's immediate central emphasis is on the d4 square, and, if White foregoes playing d4 (as for instance in the various "closed" variations), then Black's control over this square continues.

**DIAGRAM 24**

BLACK

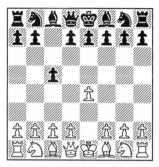

WHITE

*Sicilian Defense: 1 e4 c5*

3. Since 1 ... c5 establishes a beachhead on the queenside, Black's opportunities for active play are generally on that side.

4. In normal variations White plays an early d4—usually on the third move. After Black exchanges pawns with ... cxd4, the c-file is then half-open, and this file becomes Black's primary attacking route on the queenside.

5. White's e-pawn is strongly placed on the fourth rank. If Black can get in ... d5 to eliminate White's e-pawn *with no resulting disadvantages,* he obtains full equality. Therefore, aiming for ... d5 becomes Black's chief strategic objective. However, it is rarely possible to achieve this early in the game.

Of course, 1 ... c5 also entails some disadvantages—otherwise it would be the only opening played! These disadvantages are:

1. Black ignores White's very strong and active pawn on e4, enabling White to build up strong attacking chances on the kingside.

2. 1 ... c5 is not really a primary developing move. The only piece whose development it furthers immediately is the queen. It contributes nothing toward the development of the kingside, the area where White is expected to attack.

3. By allowing White to set up a strong attacking formation on the kingside, Black risks succumbing to a sudden mating assault. In

the early stages of the game Black is in considerably greater practical danger than White, since an attack on the king can be decisive far more quickly than an attack against a queenside point.

In general, White tries for an attack on the kingside in the Sicilian and Black for one on the queenside. Black must both parry White's attack and create counterplay for himself on the queenside. If he is successful, he has good chances of winning any endgame that results. White has good prospects of scoring with an early kingside attack.

It must be emphasized that, even though it is fully sound theoretically, the Sicilian Defense is difficult to handle in practical play. A bit of carelessness in defending and the king is lost! It is actually much better suited for a Fischer than for his many imitators and followers. Nevertheless, it is a very important opening, and I will try to present its principles as clearly as possible so that the reader, using his brave heart and the information gleaned from this book, can successfully navigate its invariably muddy waters.

# SECTION 2. Basic Principles

The main moves and their significant alternatives are as follows:

**1 e4 c5**

**2 Nf3**

The king knight is developed to its preferred central location, furthering prospects for early castling and preparing the active and developmental d4. Note that in developing the kingside minor pieces, it is more effective to develop the king knight first and only then the king bishop. There is a rule of thumb, valid most of the time (including here) that says "knights should be developed before bishops." It is easy to understand its application to our second move. The king knight's best square is f3, and there is absolutely no disadvantage in playing it there on the second move. On the other hand, the best location for the king bishop is as yet uncertain. Depending on Black's play—and one's own taste—it could belong on e2, d3, c4 or b5. Move two is too early to tell.

By any standard of chess evaluation, 2 Nf3 is a perfect move. It is the most popular move, and in master chess is played more than

75 percent of the time. Thus it follows that in almost one quarter of the games, something else is chosen. These alternatives can be divided into the categories of secondary alternatives and primary alternatives.

Following are the *secondary* alternatives and then the *primary* alternatives. We will then return to the main line:

**2 b3** White plans to fianchetto his queen bishop to bear down on the central diagonal a1-h8. This kind of a strategic approach does not mix well with the immediate activity envisioned by 1 e4, and Black equalizes with normal sound play, starting with either 2 ... Nc6, 2 ... d6 or 2 ... e6.

**2 b4** The so-called Wing Gambit, whereby White takes drastic measures to eliminate Black's c-pawn. Black should capture 2 ... cxb4, and then, after either 3 a3 or 3 d4, respond with the central advance 3 ... d5!. This way Black achieves full equality.

**2 c4** White pays primary attention to preventing Black's potential ... d5 advance and is willing to lock in his king bishop and weaken his control of d4 in order to do so. The resulting positions often occur also in the English Opening when White follows 1 d4 with an early e4. Black's most effective plan is to grab what White has voluntarily given up: control of d4. Consistent development now would be: 2 ... Nc6 3 Nc3 g6 4 g3 Bg7 5 Bg2 d6 6 d3 Nf6 7 Nge2 0–0 8 0–0, and now 8 ... Ne8! both to control d4 and to have the option of countering White's kingside play with a timely ... f5.

**2 d3** White shows his interest in a "closed" formation, but this move generally has no independent significance and leads to the positions considered after 2 Nc3.

**2 f4** Prior to playing Nf3, White advances his f-pawn both to control e5 and to be in a position for later activity along the f-file. But this move does nothing to further development and weakens the kingside. Black's most effective plan is to aim for the liberating ... d5, either after the preparatory 2 ... e6 or the immediate 2 ... d5. Then, after 3 exd5 Qxd5 4 Nc3 Qd8 5 Nf3 Nf6, Black has approximate equality because as a result of 2 f4, White is a tempo behind in development and his f-pawn is somewhat weak.

**2 g3** White aims for the immediate fianchetto of his king bishop, but the lack of attention paid to d5 allows Black the immediate 2 ... d5!. After 3 exd5 Qxd5 4 Nf3 Bg4! 5 Bg2 Qe6+ 6 Kf1 the uncastled location of White's king gives Black fully equal counterchances.

**2 Ne2** An awkward-looking move but perfectly playable if White intends to follow up with an early d4. There simply is no way that Black can immediately exploit the knight's location. Inferior now is 2 ... Nf6 3 Nbc3 d5?!, because after 4 exd5 Nxd5 5 Nxd5 Qxd5 6 d4! cxd4 7 Qxd4 Qxd4 8 Nxd4 White's edge in development gives him a significant initiative.

**2 Bc4** It is premature to place the bishop here, since after 2 ... e6!, not only is its anticipated diagonal action inhibited, but after ... d5 White will have to lose a tempo (one unit of time) to move it again.

There are three *primary* alternatives to 2 Nf3:

**2 c3** With the logical idea of building a strong center after 3 d4 cxd4 4 cxd4 Black can try to build his own center with 2 ... e6 3 d4 d5, though he must then accept an isolated d-pawn after 4 exd5 exd5 because... Qxd5?! allows White too strong a central influence after 5 Nf3. Or Black can aim to challenge White's center by 2 ... Nf6 3 e5 Nd5 4 d4 cxd4 5 cxd4 d6 6 Nf3 Nc6. In either case, with careful play Black can be expected to equalize.

**2 d4** This leads to the Smith–Morra Gambit after 2 ... cxd4 3 c3 dxc3 4 Nxc3. Theoretically, this gambit is not quite sound since for his pawn White only gains the equivalent of one developing move. But in a practical game unwary opponents can go quickly under. Black's most effective plan is to combine central influence with rapid kingside castling. The suggested approach is: 4 ... Nc6 5 Nf3 d6 6 Bc4 e6! 7 0–0 Be7 8 Qe2 Nf6 9 Rd1 e5! (planning 10 ... Bg4, which would then threaten 11 ... Nd4) 10 h3 0–0. Black then will complete the development of his minor pieces via 11 ... B–e6! no matter whether White plays 11 Be3 or 11 Bg5. Black's position then is sound and solid, and White has to prove he has some compensation for the sacrificed pawn.

**2 Nc3** This can transpose back into main lines, but its independent significance can be seen after the further moves 2 ... Nc6 3 g3 g7 4 Bg2 Bg7 5 d3 d6

This is the basic starting point of the Closed Variation. Note how White, by choosing a move order starting with 2 Nc3, has prevented Black's ... d5. Despite the closed, innocuous appearance of this position, White's prospects still lie on the kingside and Black's on the queenside. Among top players, former world champion Boris Spassky has had many successes on the White side.

### DIAGRAM 25

**BLACK**

**WHITE**

*Sicilian Defense, Closed
Variation, after 5 ... d6*

White has a number of choices for his 6th move, and formerly 6 Be3, 6 Nge2 and 6 Nh3 were all regularly played. Currently, however, 6 f4! is thought to be the most effective preparation for the intended kingside play. Black should then choose a system that allows him to retain control of his strong point—the d4 square—while also permitting a flexible response to White's kingside play. Recommended, therefore, is 6 ... e6! 7 Nf3 Nge7! 8 0–0 0–0, since Black is always ready to counter White's g4 with ... f5!.

Diffident play by Black can lead quickly to disaster. Instructive is Spassky–Geller, 6th match game, 1968: 6 f4 Nf6?! 7 Nf3 0–0 8 0–0 Rb8 9 h3! b5 10 a3! a5 11 Be3 b4 12 axb4 axb4 13 Ne2 Bb7 14 b3! Ra8 15 Rc1! Ra2 16 g4! Qa8?! (better was 16 ... e6 or 16 ... Nd7) 17 Qe1! Qa6 18 Qf2 Na7?! (better was 18 ... Nd7) 19 f5! Nb5 20 fxg6 hxg6 21 Ng5 Na3 22 Qh4! Rc8 23 Rxf6! exf6 24 Qh7+ Kf8 25 Nxf7! Rxc2 (after 25 ... Kxf7, decisive is 26 Bh6 Rg8 27 Nf4!) 26 Bh6! Rxc1+ 27 Nxc1 Kxf7 28 Qxg7+ Ke8 29 g5! f5 30 Qxg6+ Kd7 31 Qf7+ Kc6 32 exf5+ Black resigns.

We return now to the main line after 1 e4 c5 2 Nf3.

### 2 ... d6

We shall use this flexible, popular and perfect move in our main line. This pawn move guards the key e4 square (thereby enabling ...

## DIAGRAM 26

BLACK

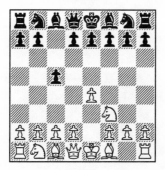

WHITE

*Sicilian Defense, Main Line,*
*after 2 Nf3*

Nf6 to be played without having to worry about White playing e5),
opens the diagonal of the queen bishop and entails no tactical or
strategic deficiencies.

Of the possible alternatives, two are perfect and the others
mediocre or inferior in various ways.

Downright poor is the immediate 2 ... d5? because after 3 exd5
Qxd5 4 Nc3 Qd6 5 d4 cxd4 White's superior development will lead
to a lasting initiative after either 6 Nxd4 or 6 Qxd4.

In the *mediocre* category are:

**2 ... a6** The hope behind this move is that White will continue
automatically with 3 d4?!, whereupon Black, after 3 ... cxd4 4 Nxd4
Nf6 5 Nc3 e5 6 Nb3 (or 6 Nf3) 6 ... Bg4!, achieves smooth development of his kingside and easy equality. Unfortunately, any reasonable third move by White, such as 3 c4 or 3 c3, stamps Black's 2 ...
a6 as a loss of time and ensures White a steady edge.

**2 ... g6** Aims for the immediate fianchetto of the king bishop.
Strategically the fianchetto is a perfectly sound idea (see our discussion of the Dragon Variation in Chapter 6), but at the moment 3
d4 is annoying, since 3 ... exd4 allows 4 Qxd4 with an attack on the
king rook.

**2 ... Nf6** This idea of Nimzovich's is analogous to Alekhine's
Defense (1 e4 Nf6) but is not as effective here since after 3 e5 it has

been shown that the move … c5 is less useful for Black than Nf3 is for White.

Black's two *perfect* alternatives are:

A) **2 … Nc6** Strategically the most logical follow-up to 1 … c5: the queen knight is developed to its preferred central location, where it bears down on the key d4 and e5 squares. There is strategically or tactically *nothing* wrong with this move; it does, however, preclude Black from playing certain currently popular variations such as the Najdorf and the Dragon. If Black continues with an early … d6, then the same variations can occur as from 2 … d6. The discussion of Black's 5th move will make this clear.

The main independent lines that can occur after 2 … Nc6 are: a) the Accelerated Dragon after 3 d4 cxd4 4 Nxd4 g6; b) the Taimanov after 3 d4 cxd4 4 Nxd4 e6; c) the Sveshnikov–Lasker after 3 d4 cxd4 4 Nxd4 Nf3 5 Nc3 e5. All of these are currently receiving extensive theoretical and practical testing.

B) **2 … e6** Black protects the key d5 square and opens the diagonal for his king bishop. From the standpoint of opening principles, the move must be rated perfect. If Black follows up with … d6, then the same variations can occur as after 2 … d6. If Black follows up with … Nc6, then the same variations can occur as after 2 … Nc6.

The most important independent line is the New Taimanov, which results after 3 d4 cxd4 4 Nxd4 a6. It looks somewhat extravagant to me but is a popular guest in tournament play.

### 3 d4

The most active and best move, successfully tested in thousands of master games. White opens both the queen bishop's diagonal and the d-file for the queen and, after the exchange of pawns in the center, will have the opportunity for active deployment of all the minor pieces. Since Black's first move has done nothing for his kingside development, rapid development of White's pieces will naturally give him good attacking chances against Black's king.

Grandmaster Bent Larsen of Denmark has made the perceptive remark that he does not really trust the accepted popular value of 3 d4 because White voluntarily offers the strategically very valuable d-pawn in exchange for Black's less valuable c-pawn. This analysis is true insofar as static strategic considerations apply. However, the specific dynamic situation must always be also considered. Here the dynamics cry out for an early opening of the position so that the inherent strength of 1 e4 can be exploited.

Instead of 3 d4, White has two other good moves:

A) **3 Nc3** The queen knight gets developed to its best square immediately. Black can't take advantage of the omission of 3 d4 by playing 3 ... e5?! since this allows White's king bishop to gain a very powerful diagonal after 4 Bc4. Black has therefore nothing better than 3 ... Nf6 or 3 ... Nc6, and after 4 d4 the game enters normal channels via transposition of moves.

B) **3 Bb5+** Up until about 1970 this was thought to be a rather amateurish check, the continuation invariably being 3 ... Bd7 4 Bxd7+ Qxd7 5 0–0. Even though White has castled rapidly, the exchange of bishops has significantly decreased White's firepower, and Black equalizes rather easily. But the whole perspective on this check changed dramatically when the superficially logical 5 0–0 was replaced with the strategically motivated 5 c4!.

**DIAGRAM 27**

BLACK

WHITE

*Sicilian Defense, after 3*
*Bb5+ Bd7 4 Bxd7 Qxd7 5 c4*

This is one of the great many variations that have been rehabilitated as a result of a deeper fundamental understanding of basic principles. The point of 5 c4 is to gain a very strong grip on the important d5 square. Since the light-squared bishops have been exchanged, White will not have to worry about his king bishop being locked in behind his own pawn formation. Thus, 5 c4 has no strategic deficiency. It also poses no tactical problems, since master practice has shown that the attempt to win a pawn with 5 ... Qg4? 6 0–0 Qxe4 leads to a decisive edge in development for White after 7 d4!. If Black develops routinely, then White will castle and play d4. If Black tries to prevent d4 by playing 5 ... e5, then White will be left with the strategically superior bishop, since Black's pawns will tend to hem in his king bishop. The overall evaluation of the position after 5 c4 is that White has a small but pleasant advantage entailing little risk.

Therefore, Black has been trying out various other defenses, including 4 ... Nxd7 instead of 4 ... Qxd7, as well as 3 ... Nc6 and 3 ... Nd7 in response to 3 Bb5+. But in every case White can expect some initiative, and thus 3 Bb5+ is a fully viable alternative to 3 d4.

### DIAGRAM 28

**BLACK**

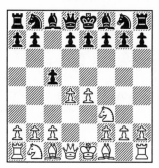

**WHITE**

*Sicilian Defense, after 3 d4*

**3 ... cxd4**

Black is not *forced* to capture, but why shouldn't he? As discussed earlier, he exchanges his c-pawn for White's valuable d-pawn and opens his side of the c–file for potential pressure by his queen rook and queen against White's queenside.

**4 Nxd4**

By far the most usual recapture. Here we have one of the rare instances where the apparently premature queen development, 4 Qxd4, is also playable. This is so because the normal 4 ... Nc6 can be met by 5 Bb5, and even though White will have to exchange off his king bishop, the resulting rapid development and retention of the queen in the center of the board gives him fully satisfactory prospects. If Black prepares ... Nc6 with either 4 ... a6 or 4 ... Bd7, White plays 5 c4, and his increased central influence compensates for the tempo lost in retreating the queen after 5 ... Nc6. Black, in theory, does have a shade easier task in equalizing against 4 Qxd4 than against 4 Nxd4, but in practice 4 Qxd4 remains a perfectly reasonable alternative.

### 4 ... Nf6

Why not? The king knight is developed to its preferred square with a gain of time because it attacks the e-pawn. The move is so perfect—not entailing even the smallest disadvantage—that there is *no* justification for playing anything else.

### 5 Nc3

Developing the queen knight to its preferred square while doing the necessary job of protecting the e-pawn is by far White's best move. Of course, the e-pawn can be protected with 5 f3, but why use a non–developing move for this when a fine developing one is available?

At first glance the developing 5 Bd3 may also seem reasonable. But it suffers from a number of defects: 1. Remembering the adage that knights should be developed before bishops again reminds us that it is still too early to know where the king bishop is placed best; 2. On d3 the bishop looks like an overgrown pawn and has no foreseeable offensive prospects; 3. By playing now 5 ... Nc6 Black gains an important tempo for development, since White's knight on d4 is unprotected.

The position after 5 Nc3 is the single most important basic position in the Sicilian Defense because four very important variations begin at this point.

Black has four perfect moves here. Three of them are easily derived from the basic principles of opening play. The fourth has been examined and proven sound in a colossal amount of analysis and practical play. These four perfect moves (variations) are:

**DIAGRAM 29**

BLACK

WHITE

*Sicilian Defense, after 5 Nc3*

### A) 5 ... Nc6

From the viewpoints of development and center control, this is a perfect move. The queen knight is developed to its preferred location without incurring the slightest inconvenience. The particular variation that results will depend on White's build-up. If he plays 6 Be2, Black can transpose into Scheveningen lines with 6 ... e6 or into the Dragon with 6 ... g8. The active 6 Bc4—for many years the line Bobby Fischer played exclusively—brings about the Sozin Variation. Black's steadiest reply to this is 6 ... e6, cramping White's king bishop.

White's most active and promising plan is the Richter–Rauser Attack with 6 Bg5, which both prepares White for queenside castling and makes it more difficult for Black to develop his kingside smoothly. The move 6 ... g6?! allows White to ruin Black's pawn formation with 7 Bxf6, while 6 ... e6 voluntarily pins Black's king knight.

Still, the latter is Black's best move, and after 7 Qd2 Black has a fundamental choice to make. He can accept a solid, though somewhat passive, position after 7 ... Be7 8 0–0–0 0–0, or he can go in for immediate counterplay with 7 ... a6 8 0–0–0 Bd7 9 f4 b5. The latter approach is currently more popular, though also unquestionably much more risky.

Note that the same position can be reached by the alternate move order 2 ... Nc6 3 d4 cxd4 4 Nxd4 Nf6 5 Nc3 d6.

### B) 5 ... e6

This move establishes the Scheveningen Variation, named after the Dutch town where the variation first gained popularity in tournament play. The Scheveningen is Black's most solid way of handling the inherently unbalanced Sicilian. The e-pawn guards the important d5 square and enables Black to play ... Be7 followed by kingside castling. White, for his part, can also develop simply with 6 Be2 and 7 0–0, a course favored by Karpov. Alternatively, White can try to take advantage of the fact that Black has voluntarily locked in both bishops by playing the centrally sharp 6 f4 or the flanking super-sharp 6 g4!?, an idea by grandmaster Paul Keres.

Note that the same position can be reached by the alternate move order 2 ... e6 3 d4 exd4 4 Nxd4 Nf6 5 Nc3 d6.

### C) 5 ... g6

Black will fianchetto the king bishop so that it bears down on the center and will bring his king to safety by castling kingside. This is the popular and important Dragon Variation. The Dragon makes strategic sense, is theoretically sound and leads to interesting tactics. It will be the variation considered in detail in Chapter Six, "Advanced Play."

### D) 5 ... a6

This is the world–famous Najdorf Variation, named for the Polish–Argentinian grandmaster Miguel Najdorf, who popularized it after World War II. It was, however, Bobby Fischer who made it famous as a result of his never–ending advocacy and successes with it. We know that it is sound because of an immense amount of analytical work done by Fischer and his army of Najdorf fans.

Let us look now at 5 ... a6 as it relates to the present situation on the board. It guards the b5 square so that neither White's king bishop nor either of White's knights can use it. Additionally, Black prepares to play a timely ... b5. This is all that it does. Are these of

## DIAGRAM 30

BLACK

WHITE

*Sicilian Defense, Najdorf*
*Variation, after 5 … a6*

substantial importance? No, they are not. Does the move do any-thing to further Black's development, central control or prospects of castling? No, it doesn't.

What this move does is to offer White a psychological challenge to "come and get me." Black is playing the already risky Sicilian almost a whole tempo down (5 … a6 is a *shade* better than making no move at all). As I said earlier, the Najdorf is sound theoretically. Sound, that is, for a Fischer or someone equally well versed in reams of recent analysis. It is extremely difficult for anyone else to play because the variations are based not so much on strategic prin-ciples as on specific, sharp, complicated "blow by blow" calcula-tions. The average player employing the Najdorf assumes a considerably greater than average risk with less than an average hope of success. Remember that Black is playing almost a whole move behind!

What can White do against the Najdorf? Obviously, many things. At one extreme, he can ignore it and develop with 6 Be2 followed by kingside castling. Anatoly Karpov plays in this way, saying, in effect, that there is absolutely no reason to give Black any of the hoped–for counterchances. At the other extreme, White can imme-diately go after Black's king with 6 Bg5 e6 7 f4. Variations emanating from 6 Bg5 are extremely complicated, tactical, long, difficult—and continually changing. Middle ground possibilities include such continuations as 6 a4 and 6 f4.

Besides the "perfect four" discussed above, all other Black moves are inferior. I will make special mention only of 5 ... e5?! because it is a favorite among many amateurs.

**DIAGRAM 31**

BLACK

WHITE

*Sicilian Defense,*
*after 5 ... e5?!*

This move finds favor because, I guess, it looks good to some: White's king knight is driven from its central location, and the pawn on e5 is centrally more active than it would be on, say, e7. But the disadvantages of the move are severe. First of all, Black *permanently* weakens his important d5 square, since he no longer has a pawn available to protect it. Second, the d-pawn on d6 will be backward and vulnerable to an attack on the d-file. Moreover, Black's king bishop is sentenced to a life of dreary passivity. On e7 it has no scope and functions mostly to protect the e-pawn. If it is fianchettoed (placed on g7), it also has few prospects, since the Black pawn on e5 severely limits its scope. Additionally, with the bishop on g7, the d-pawn may be very weak.

White's most effective response is to take immediate advantage of the weakening of the light squares in Black's position by playing 6 Bb5+. After 6 ... Nbd7 White has 7 Nf5, and after 6 ... Bd7 White plays 7 Bxd7+ Qxd7 Nf3.

# CHAPTER 6
# *Sicilian Defense: Advanced Play*

Most variations of the Sicilian Defense do follow the logical require-ments of good opening principles. A deeper and longer look at one of them can illustrate very well the general theme of "how to play good opening moves." Moreover, such an investigation will also teach much about the strategies and tactics involved in the Sicilian. For this closer look into the Sicilian, I have selected the Dragon Vari-ation. As already mentioned in Chapter 5, the Dragon both makes a lot of strategic sense and leads to thematic, sharp tactics.

Our starting point is the position after 1 e4 c5 2 Nf3 d6 3 d4 cxd4 4 Nxd4 Nf6 5 Nc3 g6.

### DIAGRAM 32

**BLACK**

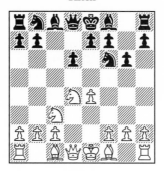

**WHITE**

*Sicilian Defense, Dragon
Variation, after 5 ... g6*

The most important characteristics of the Dragon from the points of view of both White and Black are:

1. The obvious follow-up to 5 ... g6 is to fianchetto the king bishop by ... Bg7 so that it exerts pressure along the center diagonal. Since Black is ready for kingside castling as soon as ... Bg7 has been played, the kingside is the logical place for Black's king.

2. The central pawn formation is in White's favor, since his e-pawn on e4 controls more space than Black's d-pawn on d6. As is generally true in the Sicilian, if Black can play ... d5 without disadvantage, he will have sound equality.

3. The move 5 ... g6 has slightly but fundamentally weakened Black's kingside, since Black's g-pawn can now be attacked by a White h-pawn on h5. This in turn will lead to the opening of a file on the kingside, most likely the h–file.

4. White has the option of castling on either side. Of course, castling kingside is inherently safer. However, the queenside is reasonably safe on a short-term basis, and castling there allows White the prospects of an attack against Black's kingside. The key elements in this attack are the opening of the h–file and the exchanging off of Black's king bishop via Bh6.

Let us now look at the Dragon Variation's main lines and significant alternatives. From the starting point of Diagram 32, the play develops as follows:

**6 Be3**

With both Knights developed, White's next goal is to bring out the bishops. The queen bishop seems to have two logical posts: g5 and e3. Though 6 Bg5 looks good at first glance, the attack on the king knight is blunted by the simple 6 ... Bg7. Moreover, Black will get counterchances against White's loosely protected d4 square (i.e., the king knight). On the other hand, 6 Be3 develops the queen bishop to a flexible, centrally supportive square with no drawbacks. The move even contains a sneaky trap. If Black gets too frisky and plays 6 ... Ng4?, White's 7 Bb5+! leads to heavy gain of material after 7 ... Bd7 8 Qxg5.

White could also develop his king bishop first, placing it either on c4 or e2. But since the best square of the queen bishop is already known, it is somewhat more flexible to develop that bishop first. Play different from the main line of the Dragon usually ensues if White plays 6 f4, the Löwenfish Variation. Black's soundest counter is 6 ... Nc6, when the position after 7 Nxc6 bxc6 8 e5 Nd7! 9 exd6 exd6 offers approximately equal chances. The strategic fault of the Löwenfish is that, as can be easily seen, White's central superiority has disappeared, while Black's position remains sufficiently sound.

**6 ... Bg7**

Since this is the idea behind 5 ... g6, there is absolutely no reason not to play it immediately. From a practical standpoint, however, 6 ... Nc6 is equivalent.

**7 f3**

**DIAGRAM 33**

BLACK

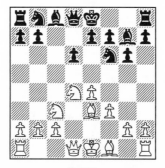

WHITE

*Sicilian Defense, Yugoslav*
*Attack, after 7 f3*

The introduction to the Yugoslav Attack. White will continue with Qd2 and castle queenside. The preparatory text move serves a number of functions: Black's annoying ... Ng5 is prevented, the e-pawn is securely protected and the potential kingside advance g5 is prepared. The Yugoslav Attack is by far the sharpest way for White to fight the Dragon and is the most popular method in master praxis.

Fully sound, however, is the so-called "old" or "normal" variation, where White castles kingside. The key position in this line arises after 7 Be2 Nc6 8 0–0 0–0. White cannot immediately attack on the king-side with 9 f4?! since Black then plays 9 ... Qb6! with a simple attack on the b-pawn and a camouflaged attack on the king knight (the threat is 10 ... Nxe4!, winning the e-pawn). Black, for his part, having castled, is ready to play 9 ... d5, a move that equalizes after 9 f3, 9 h3 or 9 Kh1 and leads to just a tiny disadvantage after 9 Qd2.

Main line play results after 7 Be2 Nc6 8 0-0 0-0 and now 9 Nb3 Be6 10 f4. Black has two methods to cope with White's planned f5. In the older Maroczy Variation Black plays 10 ... Na5 in order to continue 11 ... Bc4 after 11 f5. In the newer Tartakower Variation Black prevents f5 by 10 ... Qc8 and then aims to get in ... d5 by playing ... Rd8. In either case, Black can expect approximate equality in due course.

### 7 ... Nc6

Developing the QN to its best square is a perfect move.

### 8 Qd2

Continuing with the plan of getting ready for queenside castling.

### 8 ... 0–0

Even though it can be clearly anticipated that White will try to attack on the kingside, Black's king will still be safer there than in the center. Moreover, the king rook is brought into play and his chances for ... d5 increased. Castling queenside is not viable, since not only is the king exposed there (the c-pawn is missing!), but also Black's thematic attacking chances lie along the c-file, and the presence of his king in this sector will hamper his counterplay significantly.

### 9 Bc4

The newer and most common move. The bishop is aggressively posted to attack the f7 square and Black's freeing ... d5 inhibited. But there also is an unavoidable drawback involved: the bishop's unprotected status on c4 will allow Black to gain a tempo or two for his own development.

Also playable and good is the older 9 0–0–0. Black then has the double-edged option of 9 ... d5!?, leading to 10 exd5 Nxd5 11 Nxc6 bxc6. Analysis and practical play have shown that Black does not have to worry about losing a pawn after 12 Nxd5 cxd5 13 Qxd5 since with 13 ... Qc2! he gets excellent attacking chances along the half-open b-file and c-file (14 Qxa8?! Bf5! leads to advantage for

**DIAGRAM 34**

BLACK

WHITE

*Sicilian Defense, Yugoslav
Attack, after 8 ... 0-0*

Black). Current master thinking is that White should play strategically with 12 Bd4! e5 13 Bc5 Be6! 14 Ne4!, leading to a slightly more pleasant position for White, since after 14 ... Re8 15 h4! White still has attacking chances on the kingside, whereas Black's king bishop is dormant and the pin along the d-file can prove to be annoying.

**9 ... Bd7!**

On the face of it quite logical: the last minor piece is developed and the way freed for ... Rc8 to start counterplay along the c-file. Still it took the master fraternity a long time—over six years—to discover it! The explanation is that they were so terrorized by the apparent power of White's king bishop that it was felt *immediate* steps must be taken to neutralize its power. So Black tried 9 ... Nxd4 10 Bxd4 Be6, or 9 ... Na5, or 9 ... Nd7 followed by 10 ... Nb6 and 11 ... Na5, or 9 ... a6, or 9 ... a5—and all for naught. Since nothing exotic worked, the decision was made to go back to basics and, lo and behold, Black began to secure good chances. This is one of the best examples of how correct application of basic opening principles—completing development before starting action, the importance of central influence, etc.—could have saved many masters much grief.

**10 h4**

### DIAGRAM 35

**BLACK**

**WHITE**

*Sicilian Defense, Yugoslav
Attack, after 10 h4*

The two inherent aspects of White's future strategy are attack along the h–file and castling queenside. It probably does not matter too much whether White first plays 10 0–0–0 or 10 h4. Current master practice prefers the sharper text move, since it entails no disadvantages and immediately subjects Black to a sharp attack.

Even though White's king bishop is vulnerable on c4, that is *no* reason *voluntarily* to lose a tempo by retreating it to b3. After 10 Bb3?! Black can immediately start a promising queenside action with 10 ... Nxd4! 11 Bxd4 b5!, to be followed by ... a5. This leads to fully equal counterchances for Black, since White's king bishop occupies a precarious position. Remember: Do not waste time with unnecessary retreats when the position requires sharp play by both sides!

The text move tells Black without a shadow of doubt what is coming: a sharp, direct attack on his king. How should he respond? Two general approaches are feasible: 1) immediately to counterattack on the queenside, or 2) to try to combine counterattack with defense.

**10 ... h5**

Master practice in the early 1980s has given preference to the approach in which Black tries to slow down White's attack along the h–file. The text move does exactly that, but at a very clear and obvious cost: a fundamental weakening of Black's kingside pawn formation. Moreover, Black will be a move behind in his efforts at counterplay.

The alternative plan is to start an immediate counterattack. Since sharp, tactical sub-variations can easily gain or lose popularity, the "immediate counterattack" variations may reappear in master practice at any time. Such a variation is well demonstrated in the course of A. Karpov–V. Korchnoi, Match Game #2, 1974:

10 ... Rc8 (threatening to win material with 11 ... Nxd4) 11 Bb3 Ne5 (immediately going for counterplay along the c-file) 12 0–0–0 Nc4 13 Bxc4 (the necessity for this capture shows up the major strategic disadvantage of 9 Bc4; White's king bishop has made two moves just to be exchanged for Black's queen knight on a square that the bishop controls equally well from f1!) 13 ... Rxc4 14 h5! (compared to the preparatory 14 g4, White saves one or two moves for the opening of the h–file by sacrificing the h-pawn) 14 ... Nxh5 15 g4 Nf6 16 Nde2!

### DIAGRAM 36

**BLACK**

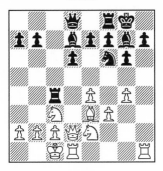

**WHITE**

*Karpov-Korchnoi 1974,*
*after 16 Nde2!*

A multipurpose move: 1) The knight on c3 is overprotected, thus making it difficult for Black to gain counterchances with the characteristic ... Rxc3 sacrifice, 2) the knight can move to g3 or f4 for attacking purposes, 3) Bh6 is threatened. The immediate 16 Bh6?! allows 16 ... Nxe4! 17 Qe3 Rxc3!, with Black having sufficient counterplay for Black.

The game continued: 16 ... Qa5 (counterattack!) 17 Bh6 (exchanging off Black's valuable offensive and defensive bishop) 17 ... Bxh6 18 Qxh6 Rfc8 (counterattack!) 19 Rd3! (again preventing the counterplay resulting from an exchange sacrifice on c3; Black should now neutralize White's attack with 19 ... Qd8 20 g5 Nh5 21 Ng3 Qf8, after which White will regain the pawn and keep a slight endgame edge) 19 ... R4c5? 20 g5!! Rxg5 (forced) 21 Rd5!! (White's 20th and 21st moves together comprise a brilliant concept for attacking Black's weak point: the h-pawn; Black is lost) 21 ... Rxd5 22 Nxd5 Re8 23 Nef4! Bc6 24 e5!! Bxd5 (White's powerful 24th move prevents a Black queen check from g5 in the following variation: 24 ... dxe5 25 Nxf6+ exf6 26 Na5! gxh5 27 Rg1+) 25 exf6 exf6 26 Qxh7+ Kf8 27 Qh8+ and Black resigned, since after 27 ... Ke7 28 Nxd5+ Qxd5 29 Re1+ he loses heavy material.

**11 0–0–0**

**DIAGRAM 37**

BLACK

WHITE

*Sicilian Defense, Yugoslav*
*Attack, after 11 0-0-0*

With his immediate attacking prospects stopped, it is quite in order for White to complete queenside development by castling.

**11 ... Rc8**

**12 Bb3**

The threat of 12 ... Nxd4 forces the bishop to retreat.

**12 ... Ne5**

### DIAGRAM 38

**BLACK**

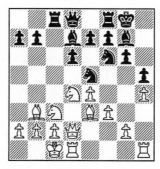

**WHITE**

*Sicilian Defense, Yugoslav*
*Attack, after 12 ... Ne5*

The critical position in this sub-variation. Black is ready to inaugurate his play along the c-file with 13 ... Nc4, whereas White's attack seems stymied. The following choices for White must be considered:

1) *Brute force*—White plays 13 g4?!: Black's position is sufficiently sound, and after 13 ... hxg4 14 h5 Nxh5 15 Bh6 e6! he has every reason to expect that he will weather White's attack successfully.

2) *Quiet preparation*—White plays 13 Kb1: Black achieves approximate equality after the thematic 13 ... Nc4 14 Bxc4 Rxc4 15 Nb3 Qc7.

3) *Strategic exchange*—White plays 13 Bh6: Though the exchange of the dark-square bishops is of strategic value to White, Black has the following tactical method of gaining full counterplay: 13 ... Bxh6! 14 Qxh6 Rxc3! 15 bxc3 Qa5 16 Kb2 Rc8. White's weakened king position and pawn structure give Black full compensation for the exchange.

White must do something, even though no truly forceful action is available. The best move is:

**13 Bg5!**

A creative change of plan. White cannot achieve anything immediately against Black's kingside, although Black's weaknesses there do give White *long-term* prospects. White therefore prepares for action in the center. Black cannot chase the annoying Bishop away with 13 ... Nh7?!, since the misplacement of the knight means that after 14 Bh6! Bxh6 15 Qxh6, the exchange sacrifice 15 ... Rxc3 does not yield full compensation anymore.

**13 ... Rc5!**

Black gets ready to start counterplay with 14 ... b5 while giving additional support to his central squares, particularly e5. The latent power of White's 13 Bg5 makes it impossible for Black to execute more conventional plans under satisfactory conditions. Thus 13 ... Qa5?! is met by 14 Kb1!, and already White threatens 15 Bxf6! Bxf6 16 Nd5, ruining Black's pawn formation. If 13 ... Nc4?!, then 14 Bxc4! Rxc4 15 Nb3!, and White threatens the annoying 16 e5! since 16 ... dxe5 leads to the loss of a piece after 17 Bxf6!.

From here on, we follow the game A. Karpov–G. Sosonko, Tilburg 1979:

**DIAGRAM 39**

BLACK

WHITE

*Karpov–Sosonko,*
*after 13 ... Rc5!*

### 14 Rhe1!?

Since White's immediate prospects lie in the central break e5, he puts maximum power behind it. Less effective is the immediate 14 f4, since after 14 ... Nc4 15 Qd3 b5 16 e4, Black gets excellent counterplay with 16 ... Qb6!. Note that White cannot win a piece with 17 exf6 since after 17 ... exf6 his queen bishop is trapped.

### 14 ... b5

Black starts his counterattack.

### 15 f4

Everything is set for the coming e5 break and there is no time to tarry.

### 15 ... Nc4

### 16 Bxc4 bxc4?

Black hopes to gain counterplay along the b-file but there will not be sufficient time for it. Therefore, correct and necessary is 16 ... Rxc4. Then, after 17 e5, Black can counter with 17 ... b4 18 exf6 exf6!. Other 17th moves for White should also allow Black sufficient counterplay. Of course, the specific possibilities can turn out to be exceedingly complicated—as is characteristic of the Yugoslav Attack against the Dragon.

### 17 Bxf6!!

Played with great insight into the position. As the note to White's 14th move shows, the queen bishop is vulnerable on g5, and White therefore exchanges it off. After the routine 17 e5?! Black would indeed get a very strong attack with 17 ... Qb6! 18 exf6 Rb8. After the text, 17 ... exf6 would lock in the king bishop and leave the d-pawn vulnerable, allowing White to gain a big edge with either 18 Nf3 or 18 f5.

### 17 ... Bxf6

### 18 e5! Bg7

There is no choice, since both 18 ... dxe5? 19 Nf3!, and 18 ... Bxh4? 19 Rh1 are totally unsatisfactory for Black.

**19 e6!**

Notice how the central advance is ultimately used for the further weakening of Black's kingside.

**19 ... Bc8**

**20 exf7+ Rxf7**

**21 Ne6 Bxe6**

**22 Rxe6 Qa5!?**

Aiming for the most counterplay possible under the circumstances. If White rushes things with 23 Rxg6?!, then after 23 ... Kh7! Black would stand reasonably well, since 24 Rg5 Bxc3 forces 25 Qxc3 with an equal endgame.

**23 Qe3!**

Increasing the pressure on Black's position *and* giving White's king a flight square on d2.

**23 ... Bxc3**

The resulting queenside attacking chances are not sufficient to compensate for the mortal weakening of Black's king position. Even after the slightly better 23 ... Bf6, White sets unsolvable problems for Black with 24 Ne4!..

**24 bxc3 Qxa2**

**25 Rxg6+ Kf8**

**26 Qe4!**

The centralized queen threatens 27 Qa8+ and is also ready to shift to the kingside if necessary.

**26 ... Qa6**

**27 Rd5!**

Exchanging off one rook allows White to break into Black's position with decisive effect. The elegant refutation of 27 ... Qc6 is 28 Rxc5!.

**27 ... Rf6**

**28 Rxc5 Rxg6**

**29 Rxh5 d5**

**30 Rxd5 Black resigns**

He is two pawns down and remains in danger of being mated.

# CHAPTER 7

# *Queen's Gambit Declined: Basic Principles*

During most of the 19th century, romanticism and attack was the order of the day, and White's first move was almost invariably 1 e4. Near the end of the century the top players realized that opening the game with 1 d4 also had much chess logic behind it. In one area there was no disagreement at all: the only correct reply to 1 d4 was thought to be 1 ... d5. The reasoning behind 1 ... d5 was (and still is) fully sound. Black imitates White's strong central move and will fight to retain control of his important d5 square. Since the queen already protects this square from its original position, Black's task in protecting d5 is considerably easier than in protecting e5 in the openings starting with 1 e4 e5. Because of its inherent soundness, the Queen's Gambit Declined has stood the test of time, and in the 1980s has the same good reputation as it enjoyed one hundred years earlier.

The most important characteristic of 1 ... d5 followed by 2 ... d6 is its solidity. It is preferred by masters who are quite willing to defend a slightly cramped position in order to achieve safe and sound equality in due course. White's play in the Queen's Gambit generally starts on the queen's side of the center. But opening the center can easily swing the scene of action to the kingside. Black's approach in general is to defend whatever area White is attacking. Black's opportunities for counterplay will usually arise whenever White has overextended himself somewhere.

Of course, specific variations have their own particular points. The main line and significant alternatives are as follows:

**1 d4 d5**

**2 c4**

White immediately attacks Black's key central outpost, the d-pawn, from the flank. This opening is called the Queen's Gambit.

## DIAGRAM 40

**BLACK**

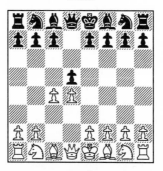

**WHITE**

*Queen's Gambit,*
*after 1 d4 d5 2 c4*

The name is something of a misnomer, however. The word "gambit" suggests sacrifice or risk, and in the Queen's Gambit White sacrifices and risks nothing. Black can capture the c-pawn, but he cannot afford to hold on to it. For instance, after 2 ... dxc4 3 Nf3 a6 4 e3 b5?! 5 a4 White is sure to recover his pawn with a greater-than-normal advantage. Two examples: 5 ... c6 6 axb5 cxb5 7 b3! cxb3 8 Bxb5+!, or 5 ... Bb7 6 b3!.

Nevertheless, 2 ... dxc4 plays an accepted role in opening theory and is called the Queen's Gambit Accepted. After 3 Nf3 Black gives back the captured pawn and tries to complete his development quickly. The two main approaches are: 1) 3 ... a6 4 e3 Bg4 5 Bxc4 e3 6 h3 Bh5 7 Nc3 Nf6 8 0–0 Nc6 9 Be2 Bd6, and 2) 3 ... Nf6 4 e3 e6 5 Bxc4 c5 6 0–0 a6 7 Qe2 b5 8 Bb3 Bb7. As can be seen, in each case Black's basic development is sound, but White has a noticeable central superiority. According to "official" opening theory, the Queen's Gambit Accepted is a fully satisfactory opening system. Still, White's central superiority, attained with little risk, suggests to me that the White side is considerably easier to handle than the Black side. The popularity of the QGA has fluctuated throughout the years. In the 1980s it was on the upswing again.

**2 ... e6**

The primary goal of 1 ... d5 is to control the important d5 and e4 central squares. Black's second move should be consistent with this plan. Completely wrong, therefore—though common in amateur chess—is 2 ... Nf6?, since after 3 cxd5 Black's thematic central influence has largely disappeared and White will soon attain a substantial central and strategic superiority.

To fortify d5 Black must play either 2 ... e6 or 2 ...c6. The more common move is 2 ... e6, bringing about variations of the so-called Orthodox Defense of the Queen's Gambit Declined. The move has the obvious advantage of furthering kingside development and castling. There is one strategic disadvantage, however: the queen bishop is locked in behind its e-pawn.

The logic behind 2 ... c6—the Slav Defense—is that d5 is supported while the diagonal of the queen bishop remains open. But there is a small problem with the Slav also: after 3 Nc3 Nf6 4 Nf3, how is Black to develop his king bishop? If now 4 ... e6, the queen bishop is again locked in, whereas 4 ... g6 leads to a passive variation of the Grünfeld Defense (1 d4 Nf6 2 c4 g6 3 Nc3 d5). The development of the queen bishop with 4 ... Bf5, although it may appear logical, unfortunately leads to difficulties with the protection of the queenside after 5 cxd5! cxd5 6 Qb3!. So Black has nothing better than to give up the center by 4 ... dxc4.

The redeeming factor for Black in this is that White cannot smoothly recover his pawn with the desirable 5 e3 or 5 e4 because, under the changed circumstances, Black can play 5 ... b5 with good effect. Therefore, White must prevent that move by first playing 5 a4, but that move has two drawbacks: one tempo is lost, and the b4 square is permanently weakened. These factors allow Black to achieve a satisfactory position as follows: 5 ... Bf5 (to control e4) 6 e3 e6 (to develop the kingside) 7 Bxc4 Bb4 (to develop the Kingside and control e4 indirectly) 8 0–0 0–0 9 Qe2 Nbd7 (completing the development of the minor pieces).

This is a key position in the Slav Defense. White has a central advantage and can enhance it after 10 e4 Bg6. But Black's position is very solid and his minor pieces well developed. Thus Black's ultimate disadvantage is just a small one.

**3 Nc3**

## DIAGRAM 41

**BLACK**

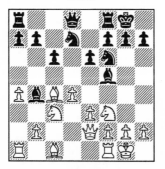

**WHITE**

*Slav Defense, after 9 ... Nbd7*

From the standpoint of strategic principles the most logical follow-up. The queen knight is immediately developed to its ideal square, where it attacks d5 and protects e4. Although from a practical standpoint 3 Nf3 is about equivalent, 3 Nc3 is thought to be a shade more accurate, since Black's d-pawn is under pressure and White retains more flexibility in the immediate future. That is, Nc3 is important to all of White's possible plans, whereas the development of the king knight may be delayed in certain variations.

### 3 ... Nf6

In every respect a perfect move: the king knight is developed to its ideal square, protecting d5 and enabling Black to castle rapidly.

There are two other possibilities that occur often in master chess. The first is 3 ... Be7, a sophisticated way of preventing White's immediate Bg5, which, however, is only significant if White intends to play the Exchange Variation (cxd5 on the 3rd, 4th or 5th move). I'll have more to say about this a bit later on.

Black's second alternative is a major one: 3 ... c5, leading to the Tarrasch Defense of the QGD. In exchange for an isolated queen pawn, Black obtains free piece play and good central presence. The popularity of the Tarrasch has had many ups and downs, and in the 1980s was on the upswing again. Among recent world champions,

Boris Spassky sometimes played it. The main line variation occurs after 4 cxd5 exd5 5 Nf3 Nc6 6 g3! Nf6 7 Bg2 Be7 8 0–0 0–0.

**DIAGRAM 42**

BLACK

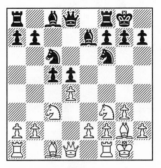

WHITE

*Tarrasch Defense,*
*after 8 ... 0–0*

White has developed his king bishop so that it is trained on Black's isolated d-pawn. The normal moves for White now are 9 dxc5 and 9 Bg5, and with either one he can expect a slight advantage. On the other hand, Black's development is sound and his prospects no worse than in other defenses to the Queen's Gambit.

**4 Nf3**

Developing the king knight to its ideal square furthers all three opening objectives. Equally good is 4 Bg5, which after 4 ... Be7 5 Nf3 leads to our main line.

White can also choose a radically different plan, the so-called Exchange Variation: 4 cxd5 exd5 5 Bg5 Be7 6 e3 0–0 (6 ... Bf5? fails to 7 Qb3!) 7 Bd3. Though the central tension has been resolved, White retains a number of small advantages: 1) the exchange of the c-pawn for the e-pawn gives White greater central influence, 2) White's light square bishop is more active than its counterpart, 3) White has attacking chances against Black's queenside along the c-file (if Black plays ... c6, White will attack this with b4 followed by b5—this is called a "minority attack"). In general, this move order in the Exchange Variation gives White a comfortable opening advantage. However, the play takes on "drier" characteristics than in the main line and thus is not up everyone's alley.

**4 ... Be7**

### DIAGRAM 43

**BLACK**

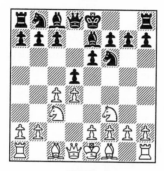

**WHITE**

*Queen's Gambit Declined,*
*after 4 ... Be7*

The standard move. Black anticipates White's Bg5 and gets ready for castling. Three significantly different plans are also possible. With 4 ... Bb4 Black enters the Ragozin Variation, a cross between the Queen's Gambit Declined and the Nimzo–Indian Defense (1 d4 Nf6 2 c4 e6 3 Nc3 Bb4). Early in his career, this was a favorite of Fischer's, although he achieved only mediocre results with it. Usually, mixing two systems achieves nothing but indigestion, and here, too, after 5 Bg5 h6 6 Bxf6 Qxf6 7 e3 0–0 8 Rc1 White has somewhat better prospects for a sustained advantage than in the main lines, mainly because Black's king bishop on b4 isn't doing very much.

Black's other two choices involve moving the c-pawn. After 4 ... c5 5 cxd5 Nxd5 (5 ... exd5 transposes into the Tarrasch), the Semi-Tarrasch Variation is reached. Unlike in the Tarrasch, Black does not have to worry about an isolated d-pawn, but on the other hand has less central influence. White can exploit this factor either by the sharp 6 e4 or the modest 6 e3, and, in each case, retain slightly superior chances.

Considerably trickier than it appears is the passive looking 4 ... c6. Its tactical point is that after the "normal" 5 Bg5, Black can capture and hold on to the c-pawn. This is called the Botvinnik Variation and leads to tremendous complications after 5 ... dxc4 6 e4 b5! 7 e5 h6 8 Bh4 g5. Chess theory has not yet given a definitive answer regarding the value of the subvariations that occur. Moreover, when White plays the strategic 1 d4, he is looking forward to a quieter life than is possible in the Botvinnik variation. Therefore, White usually responds with the modest 5 e3, voluntarily locking in his queen bishop. This brings about the Meran Variation, with the main line going 5 ... Nbd7 6 Bd3 dxc4 7 Bxc4 b5 8 Bd3. Now Black plays either 8 ... a6 or 8 ... Bb7, in each case aiming for an early ... c5. Of course, White retains some central pull after 9 e4, and with it the usual slight advantage.

### 5 Bg5

The queen bishop is developed to an active square and the attack against the knight means an indirect increase in the pressure on d5. Not as common, but also perfectly playable, is 5 Bf4. But premature is the immediate attempt at furthering kingside development with 5 e3?!, since that would unnecessarily lock in the queen bishop.

Note also that the attempt to enter the Exchange Variation now brings no advantage. After 5 cxd5 exd5 6 Bg5 c6! 7 e3 (or 7 Qc2 g6! followed by 8 ... Bf5) 7 ... Bf5, Black's queen bishop is well developed, and this is sufficient to equalize prospects.

### 5 ... 0–0!

Yes! Rapid castling is an important opening goal and is of greater necessity for Black than for White. There is absolutely no reason not to complete kingside development by castling. Pointless is the passive 5 ... c6, since Black's d-pawn is already sufficiently protected, and at some future time Black may want to challenge White's d-pawn with ... c5. It is obviously time–saving to execute that move in one step rather than two.

### 6 e3

With White's queen bishop now developed, it is in order to work on completing the development of the kingside. At this point the text move entails no disadvantages.

**6 ... h6**

The most popular move of the 1970s and 1980s. Black slightly weakens his King position, but the closed nature of the position and White's expected castling on the kingside means that the opponent will not be able to take advantage of this slight weakening. Black also has no need to fear 7 Bxf6 Bxf6, since he can readily protect d5.

From a positive standpoint, 6 ... h6 has two virtues: 1) the h-pawn is not vulnerable to an anticipated attack by White's Qc2 and Bd3, and 2) White's queen bishop is made to declare its intentions.

The time–tested alternative is the "classical" 6 ... Nbd7. This inaugurates a sound though passive plan whereby Black will slowly aim for an eventual equality. The main line is 7 Rc1 c6 8 Bd3 dxc4 9 Bxc4 Nd5; in this particular approach it is easier for Black to force piece exchanges if White's queen bishop is on g5, and therefore in this instance the move ... h6 would not be advantageous.

**7 Bh4**

It is consistent to retain the "semi-pin" secured by 5 Bg5.

**DIAGRAM 44**

BLACK

WHITE

*Queen's Gambit Declined,*
*after 7 Bh4*

This position is the starting point for a number of possible variations in the Orthodox Defense to the Queen's Gambit Declined. A comparison of the development of each side leads to the following evaluation: White, as a result of having his c-pawn on c4, has more central influence, and his three developed minor pieces work on important central squares. White's Kingside development has lagged, but the still–closed nature of the position means that his King is in no immediate danger. Black, for his part, has completed his Kingside development and brought his King to safety by castling. Moreover, his central bastion on Q4 is quite secure.

White's short–term plan is clear: he wants to complete his Kingside development. But what should Black aim for now? Actually, Black has three reasonable approaches:

1. Lasker's freeing maneuver: **7 ... Ne4.**

Black's position is somewhat cramped, of course, and the standard technique for freeing cramped positions is to exchange pieces. The text accomplishes this after the usual moves 8 Bxe7 Qxe7 9 cxd4 Nxc3 10 bxc3 exd4. But these exchanges lead to a strengthening of White's center, since his b-pawn has been transformed into a c-pawn. This factor allows White to obtain a slight advantage as follows: 11 Qb3! Rd8 12 c4! dxc4 13 Bxc4 Nc6 14 Be2. Whether Black exchanges queens or not, White will castle kingside, and his central superiority will offer him somewhat better chances.

2. The delayed classical **7 ... Nbd7.**

Now after 8 Rc1 c6 9 Bd3 dxc4 10 Bxc4, the move 10 ... Nd5?! is not efficient, since after 11 Bg3! Black has nothing to show for his decreased central influence. However, the sharper 10 ... b5!? 11 Bd3 a6, whereby Black aims to challenge White's center with ... c5 (e.g., 12 0–0 c5), gives Black prospects for eventual equality.

3. Tartakower's **7 ... b6.**

This will be our main line and will be discussed in detail in Chapter 8.

Other moves by Black are either inadvisable or downright poor. Thus 7 ... Nh5? blunders away a pawn after 8 Bxe7 Qxe7 9 cxd5, whereas 7 ... c5?! leads to an isolated and vulnerable d-pawn after 8 cxd5 exd5 9 dxc5.

# Queen's Gambit Declined: Advanced Play

Our starting point is the position after White's 7th move: 1 d4 d5 2 c4 e6 3 Nc3 Nf6 4 Nf3 Be7 5 Bg5 0–0 6 e3 h6 7 Bh4.

What is and what is not in order in Black's position? Well, he has brought his king to safety by castling, his kingside is well developed and has no noticeable weaknesses, his central influence is good. Black's only real strategic problem is the lack of scope for his queen bishop. Black's e-pawn hems in the bishop and unless White voluntarily plays cxd5, thus enabling Black to recapture with his e-pawn, the queen bishop will remain locked in for a long time to come. During the London tournament of 1922, the Polish–French grandmaster Savielly Tartakower hit on the idea of trying to do something about the "queen bishop problem" immediately by fianchettoing it. In his game against Capablanca he played:

**7 ... b6**

### DIAGRAM 45

**BLACK**

**WHITE**

*Queen's Gambit Declined,*
*after 7 ... b6*

Black's idea is disarmingly simple and completely sound: he will follow up with the centrally logical 8 ... Bb7, and the supposedly permanent problem of the queen bishop will have been solved in an instant! Since its introduction, the Tartakower Variation has been Black's most popular way of defending the Orthodox QGD. Among recent world champions who have employed it successfully are Boris Spassky, Robert J. Fischer and Anatoly Karpov.

The special practical value of the Tartakower Variation is that it combines strategic soundness with an unbalanced position. This means that not only does Black have excellent prospects for equality, but, if White does not play correctly, he can very easily get the worst of the position.

If White does nothing—that is, ignores Black's plan—his chances for an opening advantage are nonexistent. This was well demonstrated in V. Korchnoi–A. Karpov, 1978 World Championship Match, Game #1: 8 Rc1 Bb7 9 Bd3 dxc4 10 Bxc4 Nbd7 11 0–0 c5 12 dxc5 Nxc5 13 Qe2 a6! 14 Rfd1 Qe8! 15 a3 Nfe4! 16 Nxe4 Nxe4 17 Bxe7 Qxe7 18 Nd4 Rfc8!. Draw agreed. The pawn formation is almost symmetrical and the position and chances fully equal.

Therefore, to hope for an advantage, White must try to cross up Black's plan. But how?

### 8 cxd5

The only strategic drawback of 7 ... b6 is the slight yet permanent weakening of the c6 square. The idea behind the text move is to try to take advantage of this by quickly organizing pressure along the c-file against Black's queenside.

There is another sophisticated approach for exploiting the weakness of c6. It stems from Viktor Korchnoi and consists of the plan 8 Bxf6!? Bxf6 9 cxd5 exd5. It appears that White could have saved a whole tempo by playing the immediate 7 Bxf6 (instead of 5 Bh4), but this loss of time is more than counterbalanced by the creation of the weakness at c6. Though Black is allowed the two bishops, this is no advantage here because the soundness of White's pawn chain means that there is nothing vulnerable in White's position for the bishops to attack. On the other hand, White's nimble knights can be maneuvered to attack Black's d-pawn. This will force Black to play ... c6, leading to a weakened c-pawn. White will then try to work directly against this on the c-file or will open the center advantageously via e4.

Since the advent of Korchnoi's idea, there have been further small improvements in the execution of White's plan. White often plays 8 Be2 or 8 Qb3 first, in order to induce Black to play 8 ... Bb7. This way, Black's bishop is denied a potentially more useful location on e6.

For an overall appreciation of White's strategy, A. Karpov–B. Spassky, 1974 World Championship Semi-Final Candidates Match, Game #11, is a good example: 8 Be2 Bb7 9 Bxf6 Bxf6 10 cxd5 exd5 (10 ... Bxd5 gives White too great a superiority in the center) 11 0–0 Qd6 12 Rc1 a6 13 a3 Nd7 14 b4 b5 15 Ne1 (15 Nd2! and 16 Nb3 would keep White's slight advantage) 15 ... c6 16 Nd3 Nb6? (16 ... a5! equalizes) 17 a4! Bd8 18 Nc5 Bc8 19 a5 Bc7 20 g3 Nc4 21 e4! Bh3 22 Re1 dxe4 23 N3xe4 Qg6 24 Bh5! Qh7 25 Qf3 f5? (25 ... Qf5 is required for defensive purposes) 26 Nc3 g6 27 Qxc6 gxh5 28 Nd5 f4 29 Re7 Qf5 30 Rxc7 Rae8 31 Qxh6 Rf7 32 Rxf7 Kxf7 33 Qxf4 Re2 34 Qc7+ Kf8 35 Nf4, Black resigns.

### 8 ... Nxd5!

It is imperative to exchange off a pair of minor pieces, as this makes Black's defensive task considerably easier. Inferior is 8 ... exd5?! (as played by Tartakower in 1922), since after 9 Bd3! Black has no compensation for his weakened queenside. Whether Black plays 9 ... Bb7 or 9 ... Be6, White has excellent prospects both along the c-file and with a timely Ne5.

### 9 Bxe7

After 9 Bg3 Bb7! the bishop reaches the desired central diagonal, and Black will have no problems equalizing.

### 9 ... Qxe7

The only correct capture. 9 ... Nxc3? 10 Bxd8 Nxd1 11 Be7 Re8 12 Ba3 leads to a trapped knight, while 9 ... Nxe7?! places the knight in an inactive position and allows White a clear central superiority after, e.g., 10 Be2 Bb7 10 0–0 Nd7 12 Qa4 a6 13 Rfd1.

### 10 Nxd5!

It is absolutely necessary to give Black a permanent weakness—here the d-pawn. After the routine 10 Bd3 Bb7 Black is all right.

**10 ... exd5**

DIAGRAM 46

BLACK

*Queen's Gambit Declined,*
*after 10 ... exd5*

A critical position for the evaluation of the whole Tartakower Variation. Black's kingside has been developed long since and, if he succeeds in smoothly developing his queenside, then he is assured of full equality. If White continues inexactly, then the position can easily turn against him. Witness the course of the game M. Bertok–R. Fischer, Stockholm Interzonal 1962: 11 Be2 Be6! 12 0–0 c5 13 dxc5? (13 Ne5 keeps equality) 13 ... bxc5 14 Qa4 Qb7! 15 Qa3 Nd7 16 Ne1 a5 17 Nd3 c4 18 Nf4 Rfb8, and the pressure along the b–file gives Black some advantage. Fischer went on to win after 19 Rab1? (necessary is 19 Nxe6 fxe6 20 Bg4 Ra6 21 b3!) 19 ... Bf5! 20 Rbd1 Nf6 21 Rd2 g5! 22 Nxd5 Nxd5 23 Bxc4 Be6 24 Rfd1?! Nxe3! 25 Qxe3 Bxc4 26 h4 Re8 27 Qg3 Qe7 28 b3 Be6 29 f4 g4 30 h5 Qc5+ 31 Rf2 Bf5, White resigns.

**11 Rc1!**

Immediately exerting pressure on Black's weakened queenside. White need not fear 11 ... Qb4+?, since after 12 Qd2 Qxd2+ 13 Kxd2!

White's king is quite safe in the center while his pressure along the c–file is close to unbearable.

**11 ... Be6**

To solve his queenside problems, Black must soon get in ... c5 and, to play this, the d-pawn must be protected. The queen bishop is better placed on d6 than on b7 for two reasons: 1) the c8–h3 diagonal is open, whereas the a8–h1 diagonal is blocked by the d-pawn, and 2) Black's queen will be able to make good use of the b7 square.

**12 Qa4!?**

White sees that 12 ... c5 is coming, and since it cannot be prevented, he tries to establish play against Black's c-pawn once it has reached its fourth rank. The text move is an idea of grandmaster Salo Flohr's; since its introduction in the early 1930s, it has constituted the main line of the Tartakower Variation.

Nevertheless, the queen maneuver takes time, and it will hardly be well placed on its destined a3 square. Therefore the developing—though less popular—12 Bd3! is more likely to lead to the slight opening edge White has every reason to expect in the QGD. A logical continuation would be 12 ... c5 13 dxc5 bxc5 14 0–0 Nd7 15 e4! dxe4 16 Bxe4 Rab8 17 b3 Rfc8 18 Re1, with the superior queenside pawn formation and active piece placement, giving White the slightly better middlegame prospects.

**12 ... c5**

Since this is the way Black plans to free his position, there is absolutely no reason not to play this move here.

**13 Qa3**

The idea behind White's previous move. Since Black's c-pawn is pinned, White exerts definite pressure against it, requiring very exact play from his opponent. The text is much more flexible than 13 dxc5 bxc5 14 Qa3.

**13 ... Rc8**

The only satisfactory way of protecting the pawn. After 13 ... Nd7?! 14 Ba6 Black will have difficulty on the queenside.

We now follow R. Fischer–B. Spassky, 1972 World Championship Match, Game #6:

**14 Bb5!?**

**DIAGRAM 47**

BLACK

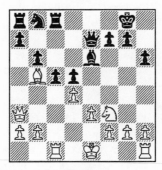

WHITE

*Fischer–Spassky,*
*after 14 Bb5!?*

An interesting, though very double-edged, plan. White tries to make it more difficult for Black to complete the development of his queenside but risks getting his bishop caught in an awkward situation. Safer is 14 Be2, after which Black's best idea is to regroup with 14 ... Qb7!, leading to approximate equality after 15 dxc5 bxc5 16 0–0 Qb6 17 Rc3 Nd7 18 Rfc1 Rcb8.

**14 ... a6?!**

A serious loss of time, since it carries no threat. Here too the most effective plan is 14 ... Qb7!, and after 15 dxc5 bxc5 16 Rxc5 Rxc5 17 Qxc5 Na6! 18 Bxa6 Qxa6 Black's edge in development is full compensation for the pawn. White does best to head for a draw with 19 Qa3 Qc4 20 Qc3.

**15 dxc5! bxc5**

15 ... Rxc5?! is met by the simple 16 0–0, parrying Black's threats while retaining the superior pawn formation.

**16 0–0 Ra7?!**

The rook does not stand well here, so it was better to chase back the bishop by 16 ... Qb7 or 16 ... Qa7.

**17 Be2 Nd7?!**

Running into another unpleasant pin. The minor evil is 17 ... c4, even though it does give White's knight a great square on d4.

**18 Nd4!**

Making it extremely difficult for Black to come up with a satisfactory plan. If, for instance, 18 ... Nf6, then 19 Nb3! Nd7 20 Rc3!, followed by 21 Rfc1 exerting very strong pressure on the c-pawn. Still, this would have been better than what happens in the game.

**18 ... Qf8?**

Unpinning the Queen, but after ...

**19 Nxe6! fxe6**

 **20 e4!**

... the looseness of Black's position is alarming.

**20 ... d4?**

A protected passed pawn is great to have—in the endgame! Here it leads to the final breakup of Black's position, since White's pieces—particularly the bishop—will now attain open lines against Black's king.

**21 f4!**

**21 ... Qe7**

**22 e5 Rb8**

**23 Bc4 Kh8**

**24 Qh3!**

Fischer is a virtuoso in playing both sides of the board. After 24 ... Rxb2 25 Bxe6 the advance of White's e-pawn and f-pawn will be decisive. Of course, what happens in the game is no better for Black.

## DIAGRAM 48

**BLACK**

**WHITE**

*Fischer-Spassky, after 21 f4!*

**24 ... Nf8**

**25 b3! a5**

**26 f5! exf5**

**27 Rxf5 Nh7**

**28 Rcf1 Qd8**

**29 Qg3 Re7**

**30 h4**

Taking the g4 square away from the knight.

**30 ... Rbb7**

**31 e6!**

Making it possible for the queen to get to e5.

**31 ... Rbc7**

**32 Qe5 Qe8**

**33 a4**

Here, and over the next few moves, Fischer marks time to demonstrate the inherent helplessness of Black's position.

**33 ... Qd8**

**34 R1f2 Qe8**

**35 R2f3 Qd8**

**36 Bd3 Qe8**

**37 Qe4!**

The beginning of the end. The threat is 38 Rf8+!. If Black tries 37
... Rxe6 38 Rf8+! Nxf8 39 Rxf8+ Qxf8 40 Qh7 mate.

**37 ... Nf6**

**38 Rxf6!**

### DIAGRAM 49

**BLACK**

**WHITE**

*Fischer–Spassky,*
*after 38 Rxf6!*

The denuding of Black's kingside leads to a rapid finish.

**38 ... gxf6**

**39 Rxf6 Kg8**

**40 Bc4 Kh8**

**41 Qf4 Black resigns**

The threat is 42 Rf8+, and 41 ... Kg8 42 Qxh6 leaves Black defenseless against 43 Rg6+ Rg7 44 e7+.

# CHAPTER 9

# *Bad Moves: How Not to Play Them*

The two general approaches in aiming for success—in business, politics, life, chess—are the positive approach and the non-negative approach. The really great achievers, of course, are those who think positively, going out and making their own successes. This is the best approach in chess, too, and that is why this book bears the positive title *How to Play Good Opening Moves*.

That doesn't mean, however, that the non-negative approach should be derided. Many people achieve perfectly satisfactory results by going along with the tide, never rocking the boat, keeping their noses clean and just not doing anything wrong.

In chess, if you don't do anything really wrong, you will come out quite well at the end. True, you won't win all your games, but the pleasant combination of many wins and some draws will always ensure a high tournament placing.

The purpose of this chapter is to help you avoid bad moves so that there will be opportunities for good ones later on. *The* principal way to avoid bad moves is to play in accordance with the opening principles we have discussed. If a move does not further at least one of the opening goals, chances are high that it will turn out to be a bad move. A helpful corollary in weeding out bad moves is to play in accordance with the basic objectives of the particular opening chosen.

A classical example of what not to do is shown in the brilliant attacking miniature P. Morphy-Duke of Brunswick and Count Isouard, Paris 1858, Philidor's Defense:

**1 e4 e5 2 Nf3 d6 3 d4 Bg4?**

The basic idea of the somewhat cramping Philidor's Defense is to protect the e-pawn with 3 ... Nd7 or the more modern 3 ... Nf6! 4 Nc3 Nbd7. The indirect defense of the pawn by pinning the knight is shown to be inferior on the very next move!

**4 dxe5! Bxf3**

Forced, as otherwise a pawn is lost.

**5 Qxf3 dxe5 6 Bc4 Nf6?**

The "Allies" do see the threat of mate in one, but they don't see White's next move. Necessary is 6 ... Qe7.

**7 Qb3!**

The double threat against f7 and b7 wins material.

**7 ... Qe7 8 Nc3!?**

Morphy by now realizes the "strength" of his opponents and has no interest in either the endgame after 8 Qxb7 Qb4+ or the superior but somewhat complicated middlegame after 8 Bxf7+ Qxf7 9 Qxb7. He is sure that sound, rapid development will lead to an even faster win.

**8 ... c6 9 Bg5 b5?**

**DIAGRAM 50**

BLACK

WHITE

*Morphy-Allies, after 9 ... b5?*

The creation of new weaknesses when already well behind in development is usually equivalent to suicide. The queenside had to be developed with the ugly looking 9 ... Na6.

**10 Nxb5! cxb5 11 Bxb5+ Nbd7 12 0–0–0**

Castling with a gain of time. At the end of this game, all of White's pieces will have had a role in his victory, whereas Black's kingside pieces will just have stood by, playing the role of spectators to the action on the queenside and in the center.

**12 ... Rd8 13 Rxd7! Rxd7 14 Rd1 Qe6 15 Bxd7+! Nxd716 Qb8+!! Nxb8 17 Rd8 mate**

Ah, you say, "But that was over a hundred years ago, and the world champion was playing against two amateurs." Yes, but as I mentioned earlier, we present-day masters are also afflicted with the disease of playing bad moves; we think we see exceptions to basic principles when in fact exceptions do not exist. In the examples that follow, I have used more recent master-level play. The point throughout is "How *not* to play bad moves."

1) *A move contrary to the spirit of the opening variation is bad.*

Example: A Karpov–A. Lutikov, Moscow 1979, Center Counter Defense:

**1 e4 d5 2 exd5 Qxd5 3 Nc3 Qd6?**

The Center Counter is in itself a shade inferior. In any case, 3 Qa5 is required, so that the queen will be safe and will immobilize White's queen knight by the pin resulting after 4 d4. On d6 the queen is nothing but vulnerable.

**4 d4 Nf6   5 Nf3 a6   6 Be3 Nc6   7 Qd2 Bg4   8 Ng5! e5?**

Allowing a cramping pawn on d5 is plainly stupid. The modest 8 ... e6 was in order.

**9 d5! Nb4   10 f3 Bf5   11 N5e4**

Gaining time by attacking the misplaced queen.

**11 ... Qd7   12 0–0–0 c6   13 dxc6! Qxd2+   14 Rxd2 Bxe4?!  15 Nxe4 Nxc6   16 Nxf6+ gxf6   17 Bd3**

Superior pawn structure, better development and the bishop pair in an open position—the combination of these advantages allows Karpov to drive Black into a hopeless situation very quickly.

### DIAGRAM 51

**BLACK**

**WHITE**

*Karpov-Lutikov,*
*after 8 … e5?*

**17 … 0–0–0   18 Rhd1 Kc7   19 c3 h5   20 Bf5 Rxd2
21 Rxd2 Nb8   22 h4 Bh6   23 Bxh6 Rxh6   24 a4 Rh8   25 b4! b6
26 b5 Rg8   27 Kc2 axb5   28 axb5 Re8   29 c4 Black resigns**

2) *Leaving your pawns unprotected is bad.*

Example: E. Sveshnikov–Buljovcic, Novi Sad 1979, KB
Fianchetto Opening:

**1 g3 c5   2 Bg2 Nf6   3 Nf3 g6   4 c3 Bg7   5 d4 0–0?**

Castling is a fine goal, of course, but pawns shouldn't be left
hanging. Correct is either 5 … dxc4 or 5 … Qb6.

**6 dxc5! Qc7   7 b4!**

Black expected that he could recover the pawn easily, but it turns
out otherwise.

**7 … a5   8 Bf4! Qc6   9 0–0 axb4   10 cxb4 Qb5   11 a3 Nc6
12 Nc3 Qc4   13 Na4 Nd5   14 Nd2 Qd4   15 Bxd5! Qxa1   16 Qb3!**

### DIAGRAM 52

BLACK

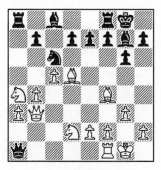

WHITE

*Sveshnikov–Buljovcic,*
*after 16 Qb3!*

To try to get back his "sacrificed" pawn, Black has had to neglect his development and compromise his queenside. By a true exchange sacrifice White gains the necessary time to exploit Black's weaknesses.

**16 ... Qf6   17 Ne4 Qf5   18 Nb6 Ra7   19 a4! Be5   20 Bxr5 Nxe5
21 f4 Nc6   22 Rd1 h5   23 Ng5 e6   24 Bg2 e5   25 Be4 Qf6
26 Rd8 Nd4   27 Rxf6 Nxb3   28 Bd5 Kg7   29 fxe5 Nd4
30 Bxf7 Black resigns**

As can be seen, Black is still playing without his queen rook and queen bishop!

3: *Weakening your king position is bad.*

    Example A) king in the center: V. Jansa–J. Arnason, Polonica Zdroj 1979, Ruy Lopez:

**1 e4 e5   2 Nf3 Nc6   3 Bb5 a6   4 Ba4 d6   5 0–0 Bd7
6 Re1 Nge7   7 c3 h6   8 d4**

Black has chosen the safe but passive Steinitz Defense Deferred variation, the primary aim of which is to safeguard (or overprotect) e5. In conformity with this idea, the next move should be 8 ... Ng6. Instead...

### DIAGRAM 53

**BLACK**

**WHITE**

*Jansa–Arnason, after 8 d4*

**8 ... g5?**

None of Black's pieces is set for an attack, and White has no king-side weaknesses, so Black's "attack" has no chance for success. The only legacy of the text move will be a chronic weakening of his own king position.

**9 dxe5!**

Opening the position to be able to take future advantage of Black's self-created weakness.

**9 ... dxe5    10 Nbd2 Ng6    11 Nf1 b5?!**

This weakening of the queenside means that Black's king will be safe on neither wing.

**12 Bc2 g4    13 N3d2 Qh4    14 Ne3 Bc5    15 g3 Qh3    16 Nb3 Bb6
17 Bd3! Nce7    18 Bf1 Qh5    19 h3!**

Black's kingside weaknesses are coming home to roost.

**19 ... Bxe3    20 Bxe3 Rd8    21 Nc5 Bc8    22 Qe2 Rg8    23 Nxa6!**

Black's queenside weaknesses are also coming home to roost. Of course, 23 ... Bxa6 allows 24 hxg4.

### DIAGRAM 54

BLACK

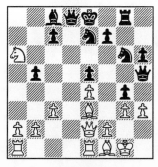

WHITE

*Jansa–Arnason,*
*after 23 Nxa6!*

---

**23 ... Nf4   24 Bxf4 Bxa6   25 Be3 Rd6   26 Rad1 b4   27 c4 Bb7
28 Bc5 Nc6   29 Bxd6 cxd6   30 c5 dxc5   31 Qb5 Ba8   32 h4 Kf8
33 Qxc5+ Kg7   34 Rd7 Qg6   35 Bc4 Rf8   36 Rd6 Nd4
37 Rxg6+ Black resigns**

Example B) castled king: A. Groszpeter–L. Hazai, 1979 Hungarian Championship, Ruy Lopez, Open Variation:

**1 e4 e5   2 Nf3 Nc6   3 Bb5 a6   4 Ba4 Nf6   5 0–0 Nxe4   6 d4 b5
7 Bb3 d5   8 dxe5 Be6   9 Nbd2 Nc5   10 c3 Bg4   11 h3 Bh5
12 g4?**

Why this horrible weakening of the kingside? With Black's king still in the center White's e-pawn is safe anyway; correct is 12 Bc2 (12 ... Nxe5? 13 Qe1!).

**12 ... Bg6   13 Nd4 Nxd4   14 cxd4 Ne6   15 f4 Bd3!   16 Rf3 Bc4
17 Nf1 c5   18 Bxc4?**

Just increases Black's central influence. After the developing 18 Be3! Black's advantage would be small.

**18 ... bxc4!   19 dxc5?! Bxc5+   20 Kg2 h5!**

Simple but strong: Black takes advantage of 12 g4?.

## DIAGRAM 55

**BLACK**

**WHITE**

*Groszpeter-Hazai,*
*after 12 g4?*

**21 Qa4+ Kf8   22 g5 g6   23 h4 Qc8!   24 Be3 Rb8   25 Rb1 d4**
**26 Bf2 Rb4   27 Qc2 Qb7?**

27 … Qc6! wins. After the text White can defend with 28 Nd2!.

**28 f5? d3   29 Bxc4+ Nxc5   30 Qf2 Ne4   31 Qd4 c3!**
**32 Qxd3 Rxb2+   33 Rxb2 cxb2   34 f6 Kg8   35 Qd8+ Kh7**
**36 Qe7 b1Q White resigns**

4: *Paying insufficient attention to the center is bad.*

Example A. Groszpeter–M. Suba, Kecskemet 1979, Alekhine's Defense.

**1 e4 Nf6   2 Nc3**

In order to secure an advantage, 2 e5 is required.

**2 … d5   3 e5 Nfd7   4 Nxd5?!**

The liquidation of the center pawns means that White is left with
dead equality. Instead, the logical 4 d4 leads to a variation of the
French Defense if Black plays 4 … e6.

**4 … Nxe5   5 Ne3 c5   6 b3?**

The square d4 is in Black's hands and there is little to be done about it. Therefore, correct is 6 g3! followed by 7 Bg2, establishing control over d5 and preparing kingside castling.

**6 ... Nec6!   7 Bb2 e5!**

Black has a firm grip on the d4 and e5 squares—and the advantage.

**8 g3 Bd6   9 Bg2 0–0   10 Ne2 f5   11 Nc4 Bc7   12 d3 Be6**

### DIAGRAM 56

**BLACK**

**WHITE**

*Groszpeter–Suba,*
*after 12 ... Be6*

Black is better because he has the superior central influence and no disadvantages. White should now play 13 Nc3! to contest the key d5 square. After the text move, White gets ground down in the center.

**13 Qd2? Bd5!   14 Bxd5 Qxd5   15 0–0–0 Nd4   16 Ne3 Qd7   17 Nc3 Nbc6   18 Kb1 b5!   19 Rdf1 Ba5   20 f4 Rae8!   21 Qf2 exf4   22 gxf4 Rf7   23 Rhg1 Nb4   24 Rg3 Bd8!   25 Qg2 Bh4   26 Rh3 Rfe7!   27 Ncd1 Nbxc2!**

Because of Black's bind in the center, the position has become ripe for a decisive combination. If now 28 Bxd4, Black wins with 28 ... Na3+! 29 Kb2 Qxd4+ 30 Kxa3 Rxe3! 31 Rxe3 b4+ 32 Ka4 Qd7+ 33 Ka5 Bd8+, followed by mate soon.

**28 Nxc2 Re2   29 Qxe2 Nxe2   30 Rxh 4 Qxd3   31 Re1 c4
32 Be5 cxb3   33 axb3 Qxb3+   34 Nb2 Rd8!   35 Na1 Nc3+
36 Bxc3 Qxc3   37 Rc1 Qf3   38 Nc2 Rd2   39 Re1 Rxc2!
40 Re8+ Kf7 White resigns**

5: *Developing your pieces away from the center is bad.*

Example: V. Hort–M. Stean, Amsterdam 1979, Sicilian
Defense, Closed Variation:

**1 f4 g6   2 g3 Bg7   3 Bg2 c5   4 e4 Nc6**

By transposition of moves, something like the Closed Variation
of the Sicilian Defense has arisen. If White now plays 5 Nc3 or 5 d3,
everything would be "normal." However:

**5 Nh3? d5!**

In the Sicilian Defense, if Black gets in this thematic advance he
has at least equality. If 6 exd5?! Bxh3! 7 Bxh3 Qxd5 and Black has a
clear advantage. Belatedly, but correctly, Hort starts paying attention to the center.

**6  Nc3!?  dxe4   7  Nxe4 Nf3   8  Nxf3+  Bxf3   9  Nf2  Bg7
10 0–0 0–0   11 d3 Qb7   12 c3 b6   13 Bd2 Bb7   14 a3 Rad8**

**DIAGRAM 57**

**BLACK**

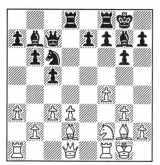

**WHITE**

*Hort-Stean, after 14 … Rad8*

The legacy of White's 5th move is that Black has greater central influence and therefore some advantage. With careful defense White is just able to hold

**15 Qa4! Na5   16 Bxb7 Qxb7   17 Rad1 Qd7   18 Qc2 Qc6 19 Ne4 Rd7   20 Be3 Rfd8   21 f5 gxf5!   22 Rxf5 Qe6?!**

22 ... Nc4! retains a slight edge.

**23 Rf3! Qb3   24 Qxb3 Nxb3   25 Nf2 Draw**

*6: Moving the same piece twice, with its second move is away from the center, is bad.*

> Example A: L. Portisch–B. Ivkov, Rio de Janeiro Interzonal 1979, Queen's Gambit Declined, Exchange Variation.

**1 d4 d5   2 c4 e6   3 Nc3 Be7   4 cxd5 cxd5   5 Bf4 c6   6 e3 Bf5 7 Nge2 Nd7   8 Ng3 Bg6   9 Be2**

**DIAGRAM 58**

BLACK

WHITE

*Portisch–Ivkov,
after 9 Be2*

The Exchange Variation has so far been handled in a slightly unusual way, but after the routine 9 ... Ngf6, Black would have a satisfactory position.

**9 ... Nf8?**

With the idea of playing 10 ... Ne6. But White is able to exploit Black's "undevelopment" with the following sharp sacrifice.

**10 h4!! Bxh4    11 Qb3! Bxg3    12 Bxg3 Qb6    13 Qa3!**

His open lines and active development give White more than sufficient compensation for the relatively unimportant h-pawn. With perfect defense Black could hold, but in practice such positions are usually lost. The game continued:

**13   ...   Ne7    14   Na4    Qd8    15   Nc5    Qb6    16   Na4    Qd8 17 Nc5 Qb6    18 Be5! f6    19 Bh2 Bf7**

Perhaps better was 19 ... Kf7!?.

**20   Bd6! Nfg6    21 Bd3! Nc8    22   Bg3    a5    23   0–0   Nge7 24 Rfe1 Rh7    25 Qc3 h4?!**

Better was 25 ... Qb4.

**26 Rab1 Qd8?! 27 Bb8! b5 28 Bxa7 Nxa7 29 b3 axb3 30 axb3 0–0 31 Ra1 Nec8 32 Bf5 Re8 33 Ra6 Qc7 34 Rfa1 Re7 35 Nd3 Be8 36 Qc5 Qb7 37 Nb4 Rc7 38 Be6+ Bf7 39 Bxc8 Nxc8 40 Rxc6 Rxc6 41 Nxc6 Black resigns**

Example B: C. Partos–V. Korchnoi, Biel 1979, Old Benoni Defense:

**1 d4 Nf6    2 c4 c5    3 d5 e5    4 Nc3 d3    5 e4 g6    6 h3 Nh5?**

Why, oh, why? The usual moves are correct: 6 ... Bg7 or 6 ... Nbd7.

**7 Be3! Bg7    8 Be2 Qb6    9 a3! Nf4?!    10 Bf3 Bd7    11 Rb1 Qa6?! 12 g3 Nh5    13 Be2 0–0    14 Nb5!**

White has a significant space advantage, and Black's pieces stand awkwardly on both sides of the board. Realizing that normal play offers few prospects, Korchnoi goes for complications and scores a lucky win.

**14 ... f5!?    15 exf5 Bxf5    16 Rc1 Nd7!?    17 g4 Be4    18 Rh2 Nf4 19   b3   Bxf3    20   Nxf3   e4    21   Ng5   Bxb2    22   Ne6!   Nxe2 23 Kxe2 Bxc1    24 Qxc1 Ne5    25 Qc3**

**DIAGRAM 59**

BLACK

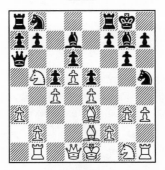

WHITE

*Partos-Korchnoi,*
*after 14 Nb5!*

25 Qc2! was a simpler win.

**25 ... Rf3!    26 Rf2! Rxh3    27 R–B4?**

27 Nxc5! wins.

**27 ... Qa4    28 Rxe4??**

28 Nxd6 was good enough for a draw.

**28 ...    Rh1    29 Qd2    Qb3!    30 Nc3    Nxc4    31 Qa2    Qxc3
32 Qxc4    Qb2+!    33 Kf3 Rh3+ White resigns**

7: *Wasting time is bad.*

Example: R. Rodriguez–L. Ljubojevic, Riga Interzonal 1979,
Queen's Gambit Declined, Tarrasch Defense.

**1 c4 c5    2 Nf3 Nf6    3 Nc3 e6    4 e3 d5    5 cxd5 exd5    6 d4 Nc6
7 Be2 Ne4!?**

Moving the same piece twice, but *toward* the center. By transposition of moves, we have reached the Tarrasch Defense to the QGD,
where, instead of fianchettoing his king bishop, White has played
e3 and Be2. This setup is less dangerous for Black.

**8 0–0 Be7    9 h3?**

Weakens the kingside while wasting time. Approximate equality is retained by 9 dxc5 Nxc3 10 bxc3 Bxc5 11 c4.

**9 ... 0–0    10 Bd3?**

Why move the king bishop again? If White wanted to put the bishop on d3, he could have played 7 Bd3.

**10 ... Bf5!    11 dxc5 Bxc5    12 Na4 Be7    13 b3 Qd6!    14 Bb2 Qg6 15 Ne1 Bxh3!    16 f3**

### DIAGRAM 60

BLACK

WHITE

*Rodriguez-Ljubojevic,*
*after 16 f3*

In the game Black played 16 ... Rad8?!, which only retained a slight edge in a subsequent endgame (17 Qe2 Ng3 18 Bxg6 Nxe2+), and, after some later blunders, Black even lost. A winning position was to be had with 16 ... Bh4! (threatening 17 ... Bxe1) 17 Qe2 Ng3! 18 Bxg6 Nxe2+ 19 Kh2 Be6!, with Black a pawn up and standing beautifully.

*8: Creating unnecessary weaknesses is bad.*

Example: P. Popovic–S. Marjanovic, Yugoslavia 1979, Sicilian Defense.

**1 e4 c5    2 Nf3 d6    3 Nc3 a6    4 g3 Nc6    5 Bg2 g6    6 d4! cxd4 7 Nxd4 Bd7    8 Nd5 e6?**

Since Black will fianchetto the king bishop, this leads to a frightfully weak d-pawn. Correct is the normal 8 ... Bg7 and, after 9 Be3, 9 ... Rc8.

**9 Ne3 Qc7   10 0–0 Bg7   11 Nxc6! bxc6   12 Nc4!**

**DIAGRAM 61**

BLACK

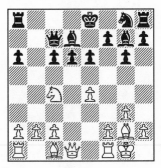

WHITE

*Popovic-Marjanovic,*
*after 12 Nc4!*

The damage wrought by Black's 8th move is now obvious. The attempt to protect the d-pawn by advancing it fails to White's brilliant sacrifice, made possible by White's huge lead in development.

**12 ... d5   13 exd5 cxd5   14 Bxd5! Rd8**

Black is defenseless after 14 ... exd5 15 Qxd5—not that what happens now is much better.

**15 Bf4 Qc5   16 Nd6+ Ke7   17 c4!! exd5   18 Nb7 Qxc4 19 Rc1 Qb5   20 Re1+ Be6   21 Rc7+ Ke8   22 Rxf7 Bf6 23 Rc7 Qb6   24 Qg4 Ne7   25 Rxe6 Qd4   26 Nxd8 Black resigns**

9: *Greedily hanging on to material is bad.*

Example: G. Sosonso–R. Hübner, Tilburg 1979, Catalan Opening.

**1 d4 Nf6   2 c4 e6   3 g3 d5   4 Bg2 dxc4   5 Nf3 a6   6 0–0! b5?!**

It is generally well recognized that in open positions king safety is of paramount importance. Therefore, grabbing stray pawns or holding on to gambit pawns is foolhardy when the position requires castling. Positions that *appear* to be closed can also quickly spring to life if the opponent has an edge in development, such as White has here. Black's attempt at retaining the c-pawn meets with a violent refutation. In order are moves such as 6 ... c5 or 6 ... Nc6, and the modest 6 ... Be7 also is reasonable.

**7 Ne5! Nd5   8 Nc3! c6?   9 Nxd5! exd5   10 e4! Be6   11 a4! b4 12 exd5! Bxd5?!**

White has steadfastly tried to open the position as much as possible. Black, for his part, must try to keep it as closed as possible. Therefore, 12 ... cxd5 is required, even though White then has the option of recovering the sacrificed pawn immediately with 13 Nxc4.

**13 Qg4!**

### DIAGRAM 62

**BLACK**

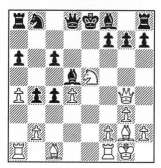

**WHITE**

*Sosonko–Hübner,*
*after 13 Qg4!*

White has a winning attack, since 13 ... Bxg2 is met by 14 Re1! and 13 ... Be6 by 14 Qh5 Be7 15 Nxc4.

**13 ... h5   14 Bxd5!! cxd5   15 Qf5 Ra7   16 Re1 Re7   17 Bg5 g6 18 Bxe7 Black resigns**

10: *Muddling around is bad.*

Example: V. Smyslov–L. Portisch, Tilburg 1979, Sicilian Defense, Najdorf Variation.

**1 e4 c5   2 Nf3 d6   3 d4 cxd4   4 Nxd4 Nf6   5 Nc3 a6   6 Bg5 e6 7 Qe2?**

The idea behind the sharp 6 Bg5 is to follow up with the central development 7 f4, 8 Qf3 and 9 0–0–0. This text does nothing for the center and inhibits the development of the king bishop.

**7 ... h6   8 Bh4 Be2   9 Bg3?**

White prevents the equalizing 9 ... Nxe4! that would follow 9 0–0–0, but in doing so he incurs an inferior position.

**9 ... e5!   10 Nb3 b5!   11 f4 0–0   12 Qd3?**

### DIAGRAM 63

BLACK

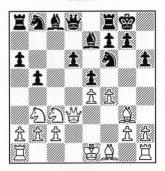

WHITE

*Smyslov–Portisch,*
*after 12 Qd3?*

What has White accomplished with his opening play? It has taken the queen bishop three moves to wind up on g3, the queen has expended two moves to stand awkwardly on d3 and the king knight has been shunted to inactivity at b3. Black has completed kingside development, started thematic queenside play and has a foothold in the center. Already Black is considerably better, and in the further course of the game he expands his advantage. White, of course, should have followed up 11 f4 with the consistent 12 fxe5.

Black won as follows: 12 ... Nbd2 13 Be2 Bb7 14 0–0 Rc8 15 Rad8 Qc7 16 a3 Nb6 17 Nd2 Nfd2 18 Bg4 Rbd8 19 Bxd7 Rxd7 20 Kh1 Bf6 21 Qe3 Re8 22 Bf2 Na4! 23 Nxa4 bxa4 24 c3 exf4 25 Qxf4 d5 26 Qxc7 Rxc7 27 Bg3 R2e2 28 exd5 Bxd5 29 Rde1 Re2 30 Rxe2 Rxe2 31 Rf2 Rxf2 32 Bxf2 Bg5 33 Be1 Be3 34 c4 Be6 35 Nf1 Ba7 36 Bc3 Bxc4 37 Ng3 Bd3 38 Nh5 f6 39 h3 Kf7 40 Kh2 Bb8+ 41 g3 Bg6 42 Nf4 Be4 43 Kg1 g5 44 Nh5 Ba7+ 45 Kf1 f5 46 Nf6 Bc6 47 h4 Bc5 48 Ke2 Kg6 49 hxg5 hxg5 50 Ke1 g4 51 Be5 Be7 52 Ng8 Bg5 53 Bf4 Bd8 54 Bd6 Kf7 55 Nh6+ Ke6 56 Bf4 Bf6 57 Bc1 Bd5 White resigns.

# CHAPTER 10

# *Castling: Early or Late?*

Rapid castling is one of the primary goals of sound opening strategy. *You should try to castle quickly.* Castling brings the following three major benefits: 1) the king is safe; 2) the castled rook is brought closer to potential action; and 3) central activity is furthered, both because the king is out of the way and because the castled rook can be used. In general, these two guidelines apply:

1) *Rapid castling is more critical for Black than for White.*
2) *Open positions—particularly those resulting from 1 e4—call for quicker castling than closed positions.*

It cannot be overstressed that in open positions the side with the uncastled king suffers from two serious problems: 1) his king position prevents the execution of otherwise logical plans; 2) his king is inherently unsafe.

Let us illustrate the first problem with a few simple examples. You are White, and the game has opened as follows: 1 e4 c5 2 Nf3 e6 3 d4 cxd4 4 Nxd4 Nf6. Black is menacing the e-pawn, and it would be nice to be able to play 5 e5, safeguarding the pawn while attacking Black's knight. Yet 5 e5 is an error, because with 5 ... Qa5 *check* Black captures the pawn for nothing. But if White had already castled, e5 would be both safe and strong.

Or consider a position commonly arising from the Exchange Variation of the Ruy Lopez: 1 e4 e5 2 Nf3 Nc6 3 Bb5 a6 4 Bxc6 dxc6 5 0–0!. The early commercial chess computers invariably played 5 ... Nf6, and after 6 Nxe5, 6 ... Qd4?! with a double attack on the knight and the e-pawn. And then after 7 Nf3, Black played 7 ... Qxe4??, noticing, *always too late,* that instead of recovering the pawn Black loses his queen to 8 Re1.

The so-called Fool's Mates—ending the game in two, three or four moves—are based on the fact that the king in the center is vulnerable to sudden attacks. In open positions, the king remains vulnerable for a long time, even if no immediate disaster occurs. The king's inherent vulnerability is well illustrated by the game E. Mednis–E. Ermenkov, New York International 1980, Sicilian Defense, Taimanov Variation:

**1 e4 c5   2 Nf3 Nc6   3 d4 cxd4   4 Nxd4 e6   5 Nb5 d6   6 c4 Nf6
7 N1c3 a6   8 Na3 Be7   9 Be2 b6**

We have entered one of the main lines of the Taimanov Variation. White has some spatial advantage, but Black's position is sound and solid. Black's usual move is 9 ... 0–0, though the immediate fianchetto of the queen bishop looks playable.

**10 0–0 Bb7   11 Be3 Ne5**

Instead, 11 ... 0–0 transposes back into known lines. By delaying castling, Black plays with fire.

**12 f4! Ned7   13 Bf3 Qc7?!**

Why doesn't Black castle?

**14 Qe2 Rb8?!**

Again, there is no reason not to castle.

**15 Rac1 h6?!**

Only after this move did it become clear to me why the Bulgarian grandmaster has avoided castling: he wants to leave his king in the center and attack my king. But this plan should *not* prove successful. White's kingside has no weaknesses, and the subsequent opening of the position will expose Black's king. With my 16th move I further safeguard my king, and with my 17th move I start to counterattack.

**16 Kh1! g5   17 Bh5! gxf4?!**

It is safer to keep lines closed with 17 ... Nxh5 18 Qxh5 Nf6 19 Qe2 g4.

**18 Bxf4 Ne5**

If 18 ... Qc5? 19 Nd5!, and after 19 ... exd5 20 cxd5! Qd4 21 Rc4 Black's queen is trapped. Black has good control of the central squares on his side of the board and thinks he is safe. White's next shot explodes this myth.

**19 Nd5!!**

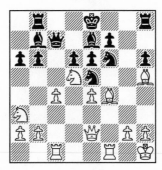

**DIAGRAM 64**

BLACK

WHITE

*Mednis–Ermenkov,*
*after 19 Nd5!!*

To get at Black's king, lines must be opened and weaknesses created in the king's vicinity. The knight sacrifice, followed by 21 Bxe5!, does this admirably.

**19 ... exd5    20 cxd5! Qd8    21 Bxe5! dxe5    22 Nc4 0–0**

With the kingside open, the chances for safety there are slight. But the king is also demonstrably unsafe in the center: 22 ... Rc8 loses to 23 d6! Bxd6 24 Rxf6! Qxf6 (or 24 ... Rxc4 25 Re6+! Kf8 26 Qxc4 fxe6 27 Qxe6) 25 Rf1 Qe7 26 Rxf7 Qxf7 27 Bxf7+! Ke7 28 Qg4.

**23 Nxe5!**

23 d6?! recovers the piece, but White wants much more.

**23 ... Rc8    24 Rcd1! Qc7**

Or 24 ... Bd6 25 Nxf7!, winning, or 24 ... Qd6 25 Nxf7! Rxf7 26 Bxf7+ Kxf7 27 e5, winning.

**25 d6! Bxd6   26 Rxf6 Bxe5   27 Qg4+ Kh7   28 Bxf7!!**

The culmination of White's attack against Black's weakened king position. There is no defense: A) 28 ... Rxf7 29 Qg6+; B) 28 ... Bxf6 29 Qg6+ Kh8 30 Qxh6 mate; C) 28 ... Bf4 29 Rxh6+! Bxh6 30 Qg6+; D) 28 ... Qc1!? 29 Qf5+ Kg7 30 Qxe5! Rc5 (30 ... Qxd1+ 31 Rf1+) 31 Rg6+ Kxf7 32 Qe6 mate.

**28 ... Qxf7   29 Qf5+ Kg8   30 Rxf7 Rxf7   31 Qxe5 Bc6 32 Qe6 R8f8   33 h3 Black resigns**

When in doubt about whether to castle, do it—the percentages are in your favor. In any abstract scheme for chess play, early castling must be given a high priority. In my consultations for and discussions with programmers of chess computers, I have always stressed the importance of getting the computer to castle early.

Of course, you as a human being, have a mind of your own and can think independently. Therefore, even though you should always give castling a high priority, castling should not be done "automatically." Sometimes castling should be postponed. We can state this in general terms.

1) *Do not castle if it is unsafe to do so.*
2) *Do not castle if there is something better to do.*

Since the primary objective of castling is to bring the king to safety, it is obviously counterproductive to castle into an attack. If your kingside is seriously weakened, castling on that side is fraught with excessive dangers. Even some weakness there should act as a flag signaling caution. Consider Diagram 65, R. Hübner–V. Smyslov, Tilburg 1979, after Black's 10th move (1 d4 d5 2 c4 c6 3 Nc3 Nf6 4 Nf3 dxc4 5 a4 Na6 6 e4 Bg4 7 Bxc4 e6 8 Be3 Bb4 9 Qc2 Bxf3 10 gxf3 0–0):

White has considerable central superiority, a spatial advantage and two potentially active bishops. Because of the likelihood that the position will be opened, White's king will be uncomfortable in the center. White should castle, but where? The safer side is the queenside, and correct is 11 Rg1! c5 12 Bh6 Ne8 13 d5 Nac7 14 0–0–0!, with a strong attacking position for White and a safe enough king. Instead, the game continued:

**11 0–0?!**

**DIAGRAM 65**

BLACK

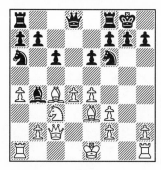

WHITE

*Hübner–Smyslov,*
*after 10 ... 0-0*

The king is uncomfortable here for two reasons: 1) the g-pawn is missing, and 2) there are few defenders nearby (unlike the situation on the queenside). There is even another reason why castling kingside is inadvisable: White can't take advantage of the open g-file to attack Black's king.

**11 ... c5! 12 d5**

After 12 Bxa6, the *zwischenzug* 12 ... cxd4! equalizes matters.

**12 ... Bxc3   13 bxc3 exd5   14 Rfd1**

Now, instead of 14 ... Qc8? 15 exd5, when White's powerful passed d-pawn gave him the advantage (White won on move 30), correct is 14 ... Nc7. Then, after 15 Bxc5 Re8 16 Be3 (16 Qa2? loses to 16 ... Nd7! 17 Bxd5 Qg5+) 16 ... Re5 17 Bf4 Rh5, Black's attacking chances against White's weakened king position give him good prospects in the middlegame.

Just because a king position is not chronically weak doesn't mean that the opponent can't launch a powerful attack against it. The prospect of such a situation should again cause us to delay castling. The course of the opening in R. Vaganian–S. Makarichev, 1979 USSR Championship, Queen's Indian Defense, is instructive.

**1 d4 Nf6   2 c4 e6   3 Nf3 b6   4 a3 Bb7   5 Nc3 d5   6 cxd5 Nxd5
7 e3 Be7   8 Bb5+ c6   9 Bd3 Nd7   10 e4 Nxc3   11 bxc3 c5   12 Be3**

If Black now plays the "logical" 12 ... 0–0?!, White can launch a
strong attack with 13 h4! followed by 14 e5, already threatening the
sacrifice 15 Bxh7+ Kxh7 16 Ng5+.

**12 ... Qc7!**

A good flexible waiting move, making White declare his plans.
In the meantime, Black's queen can find action along the c-file and
Black's queen rook can go to d1 (and Black could even castle queen-
side!).

**13 0–0 0–0!**

With White's king castled on the kingside, there are no attacking
prospects along the h-file because such moves as h4 are out of the
question. Therefore, Black can complete his kingside development
by castling there. His king is now safe and the position just mini-
mally preferable for White (because of central superiority). Black
equalized in due course, but a later error led to a 31-move loss.

If, for the moment, the uncastled king is safe, then it is all right to
ask if something else should not be accorded higher priority than
castling. The "something else" can be either defensive or offensive
in nature. For instance, it may well be in order first to prevent the
opponent from carrying out a desired defensive maneuver. A good
example is the course of the early opening in A. Gipslis–Ruderfer,
USSR 1979, Giuoco Piano:

**1 e4 e5   2 Nf3 Nc6   3 Bc4 Bc5   4 c3 Nf6   5 d3 d6   6 Nbd2 a6**

If the immediate 7 0–0?!, Black replies 7 ... Na5!, exchanges off
White's strong king bishop and obtains ready equality. White prevents this possibility.

**7 Bb3! 0–0**

Of course 7 ... Na5?! 8 Bc2 is fruitless for Black, since White
threatens both 9 b4 and the strategic 9 d4.

**8 0–0!**

Only now—but note that White still castles quite early!

**8 ... Ba7    9 Re1 Ne7    10 h3 Ng6    11 Nf1 h6    12 Ng3 c6    13 d4!**

White has delayed castling to prevent Black from exchanging pieces (see White's 7th move) and now, due to his central edge, has a clear superiority. White went on to win on move 36.

If the opponent threatens a course of action that will lead to his advantage, then it becomes even more important to delay castling. Diagram 66, V. Smyslov–O. Romanishin, Tilburg 1979, English Opening, shows the position after 1 c4 e5 2 Nc3 Nf6 3 Nf3 Nc6 4 e3 Bb4 5 Qc2 Bxc3 6 Qxc3 Qe7 7 a3 0–0 8 d3 a5 9 Be2?! (9 b3 is better) 9 ... a4.

**DIAGRAM 66**

BLACK

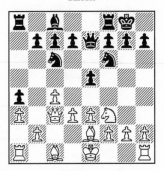

WHITE

*Smyslov–Romanishin,*
*after 9 ... a4*

As a result of White's inaccurate 9th move, Black has succeeded in fixing White's queenside (inhibiting b3 or b4). White's bishops have very little scope, whereas Black is ready for a central advance with ... d5.

Correct for White now is 10 e4!, with the following points: 1) Black's ... d5 is prevented; 2) White has a strong grip on d5; 3) a diagonal is opened for the queen bishop. Instead, White played the automatic and careless 10 0–0?!, after which Black could have gained a slight edge with the thematic 10 ... d5! 11 cxd5 Nxd5 12 Qc2 Be6, since in this position Black is more active and controls more space. (Instead, he satisfied himself with equality through the modest 10 ... d6—and still won on move 33.)

Now for some "positive" examples of postponing castling. No one is silly enough to castle when he can mate next move or win the queen for nothing. Yet there also are less obvious situations where saving the tempo required for castling is in order. How many times have we been exactly one tempo short of achieving the aims of our attack? Many times, of course. Only a very few such instances can be blamed on castling, but it is a factor always to keep in mind.

Let us follow the course of the opening in F. Trois–L. Ljubojevic, Buenos Aires 1979, English Opening:

**1 c4 e5    2 Nc3 Nc6    3 g3 d6    4 Bg2 Be6    5 d6 Qd7    6 b4 Nbe7 7 b5 Nd1    8 a4 c6    9 Ba3**

White is very strongly emphasizing the development of his queenside and consequent pressure against Black's queenside.

**9 ... d5    10 bxc6 bxc6    11 cxd5 cxd5    12 Nf3 f6**

The net result so far is that White has gained an edge in development, while Black has more pawn influence in the center. In the game White routinely continued with 13 0–0?!, and in due course had no compensation for his central inferiority. The consistent course was to work on exploiting his edge in development as follows:

**13 d4! e4    14 Nd2**

Black's last was forced. White now threatens to get to c5 via b3.

**14 ... Rc1    15 Nb5! N7c6    16 Bf8 Rxf8    17 Nb3 Nb2 18 Nb5! Nxc5    19 dxc5**

White has a promising, active position and threatens the immediate 20 Nd6+.

Finally, a game in which White demonstrates perfectly the logic of late castling. But please note that it is *White* that does it, and that we have a closed opening. The game is Schmidt–A. Kuligowski, Warsaw Zonal 1979, Benoni Defense.

**1 d4 Nf6    2 c4 c5    3 d5 e6    4 Nc3 cxd5    5 exd5 d6    6 e4 g6 7 Nf3 Bg7    8 Bg5 h6    9 Bh4 a6    10 Nd2 b5    11 a4!**

By undermining Black's queenside pawn formation, White gets c4 for his knight(s).

**11 ... b4    12 Ncb1 Qe7**

The immediate 12 ... 0–0 looks better.

**13 f3 g5    14 Bf2! 0–0    15 Be2 N8d7    16 Nc4**

Activating both knights with this and the following move. Black should now exchange one knight with 16 ... Ne5.

**16 ... Nh5?!    17 N1d2! Nf4    18 0–0!**

### DIAGRAM 67

BLACK

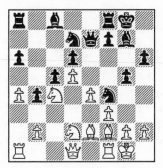

WHITE

*Schmidt–Kuligowski,*
*after 18 0–0!*

The immediate strategic goals have been accomplished and the g-pawn needed protection—so White castles!

**18 ... f5    19 Re1 Nxe2+    20 Rxe2 f4    21 e5!**

This thematic central advance ensures White's advantage. His superior development and Black's positional weaknesses mean that the sacrificed material will be recovered—sooner or later.

**21 ... dxe5    22 Ne4! h4    23 Rc1 Bh6    24 Rec2! Bxc4 25 Rxc4 Rfd8    26 Bxc5 Qf7    27 Bd6 Nb6    28 Rc5 Rd7 29 Rb5 Nc8    30 Rc6??**

A tragic time pressure error: White overlooks that after Black's reply he cannot move the attacked Bishop because of 31 ... Qxb6. White should have played 30 Rb8!, and after 30 ... Rxb8 31 Bxb8 White has Black in an absolute bind and will follow up with the decisive 32 d6!.

**30 ... Qg6! 31 Rxa5 Rxa5 32 Rxc8+ Kf7 33 Bc5 Qa6! 34 Bxb4 R7xd5 White resigns**

At this moment, it may also be worthwhile to go back to the previous chapter and review Portisch–Ivkov, where White castled late, but well, on move 23.

# CHAPTER 11

# *Pawn Play: Center,*
# *Formations, Weaknesses*

Philidor once referred to the pawns as "the soul of chess." Of course, pawn play is important, but it is only one of a number of key stratagems. Still, there is one extremely important aspect of pawn play that does not apply to any other piece: *you can't move a pawn backward!* Often you can repair a faulty queen, rook, bishop, knight or king move by simply moving that piece back where it came from. Not so with a pawn! Therefore, extreme care must be taken before a pawn is touched.

Pawn moves are notoriously poor "tempo moves," i.e., the kind of moves that maintain the status quo. This is because each pawn move inherently alters the position forever. Never *voluntarily* move a pawn, *unless you are convinced that it stands better on the new square than on its original one!*

We shall start our discussion of pawn play with the most important concepts regarding the handling of the center. Let us set up the most common position in the closed treatment of the Ruy Lopez, after the moves 1 e4 e5 2 Nf3 Nc6 3 Bb5 a6 4 Ba4 Nf6 5 0–0 Be7 6 Re1 b5 7 Bb3 d6 8 c3 0–0 9 h3.

In the Closed Variation of the Ruy Lopez, Black's immediate strategic priority is to ensure that his central bastion, the e-pawn, can hold its ground. White's last move has prepared a risk-free attack on Black's e-pawn with 10 d4. A popular continuation for Black now is the Breyer Variation ("Breyer's regrouping" would be a more accurate name).

**9 ... Nb8    10 d4**

The four primary central squares—already discussed in Chapter 1—are d4, e4, d5 and e5. Let's for a few moments limit our central evaluations to the d-file and e-file. We can arbitrarily (yet reasonably soundly) assign a value of two to a central pawn on the 4th

**DIAGRAM 68**

BLACK

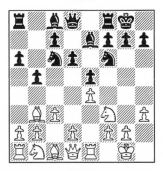

WHITE

*Ruy Lopez, Closed Variation,*
*after 9 h3*

rank and a value of one to a central pawn on the 3rd rank. Adding up the values here we get $2 + 2 = 4$ for White's central pawns and $1 + 2 = 3$ for Black's central pawns. White has more central pawn influence on an arithmetical basis (4 vs. 3) and also on a relative basis ($4 / 3 = 1.33$).

**10 ... Nbd7!**

This is Breyer's idea. But let us consider what happens if Black plays 10 .. exd4?. It may seem that Black is engaging in an equivalent exchange, i.e., giving up an e-pawn on the 5th rank for White's d-pawn on the 4th. Thus Black is left with $3 - 2 = 1$ unit of central pawns, and White is left with $4 - 2 = 2$ units. As before, the arithmetic difference is 1 unit. But there is a great change in the *relative* central influence. This now is $2 / 1 = 2$, up considerably from the 1.33 *before* the exchange. Thus, on a *relative* basis White's central influence has been strengthened considerably.

The actual situation for Black will be even worse than the above calculation shows, because White, instead of recapturing with the queen or king knight, can play 11 cxd4!. White then has $2 + 2 = 4$ units of central pawn power, whereas Black is left with only one unit. On an arithmetical basis White is ahead 3 units, and on a relative basis up by $4 / 1 = 4$! We can now easily appreciate how disastrous for Black 10 ... exd4? would be in central influence. Playing 10 ... cxd4 is called "giving up the center." *Never, never give up the center unless you have no choice or you get something valuable in return.*

### 11 Nbd2

White's normal move. What would be the result if, instead, White played 11 dxe5?!? If Black recaptured with 11... Nxe5?! then everything would be fine for White, since his arithmetic central pawn power would be $4 - 2 = 2$, while Black's would be $3 - 2 = 1$, and on a relative basis White will have increased his influence to $2 / 1 = 2$. But note what happens if Black plays 11 ... exd5!. Now the position in the center is absolutely equivalent, with each side having 2 units there. Thus the exchange 11 dxe5 by White has led to both an absolute and relative decrease in White's central power. By playing 11 dxe5 (when Black can respond with 11 ... exd5) White is said to "relieve central tension." On the face of it, this is a *disadvantageous operation. Never, ever relieve the central tension unless you have no choice or gain something valuable in return.*

After 11 Nbd7, normal variations ensue. Both sides will try to complete the development of the queenside. For quite some time to come White will try to get Black to "give up the center," whereas Black will strive to force White to "relieve the central tension."

With the above background we can understand better the rationale for the main variation of the Slav Defense that we briefly considered in Chapter 7. After 1 d4 d5 2 c4 c3 3 Nc3 Nf6 4 Nf3. Black "gave up the center" by playing 4 ... dxc4. However, he gained the following three items as compensation: 1) healthy development of his queen bishop; 2) one development tempo, since White is "forced" to play the nondeveloping 5 a4; 3) permanent control of the b5 square, which is potentially useful for the king bishop or queen knight.

The other important question is how to recapture when more than one pawn can do so. A characteristic situation is shown in Diagram 69, B. Spassky–A. Karpov, 1974 Match, Game #2, Caro–Kann Defense, after White's 12th move : 1 e4 c6 2 d4 d5 3 Nc3 dxe4 4 Nxe4 Bf5 5 Ng3 Bg6 6 Nc3 Nd7 Bd3 e6 8 0–0 Ngf6 9 c4 Bd6 10 g3 0–0 11 Bb2 f5 12 Bxg6.

### DIAGRAM 69

**BLACK**

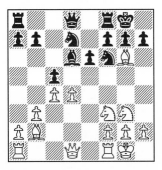

**WHITE**

*Spassky–Karpov, after 12
Bxg6*

**12 ... hxg6!**

The general principle is very clear: *always recapture toward the center unless there is a very good reason to do otherwise.* The logic is very sound: in our case the h-pawn is transformed into a g-pawn, and the control over the secondary central square f5 is strengthened. Moreover, Black's pawn formation remains sound. In this situation 12 ... fxg6?! would have two disadvantages: central influence is lessened and Black is left with an isolated and vulnerable e-pawn.

In the type of position shown in Diagram 69, there would be two situations when recapture with the h-pawn would be inferior: 1) if White could launch a strong attack along the h–file by doubling major pieces there, 2) if Black could make extremely good use of the opening of the f-file. Since these conditions are not present here, the only correct recapture is "toward the center."

The game was agreed a draw after the further moves 13 Re1 Qc7 14 dxc5 Bxc5 15 Qc2 Rfd8 16 Ne4 Nxe4 17 Qxe4—though White remains with a slight advantage.

The kind of situation where it is more useful to recapture *away* from the center is shown by the course of the game Y. Dorfman–Svedchikov, USSR 1978, Benoni Defense:

1 d4 Nf6   2 c4 c5   3 d5 e6   4 Nc3 exd5   5 cxd5 d6   6 Nf3 g6
7 e4 Bg7   8 Bg5 h6   9 Bh4 g5?!   10 Bg3 Nh5   11 Bb5+ Kf8
12 e5! Nxg3

**DIAGRAM 70**

BLACK

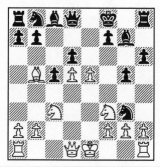

WHITE

*Dorfman–Svedchikov,*
*after 12 … Nxg3*

**13 fxg3!**

White, with his 11th and 12th moves, has launched a direct attack
against Black's king. Recapturing with the f-pawn is the only logical follow-up, since White will now have the open f-file to attack
Black's uncastled king. In the event of the "strategic" 13 hxg3?,
Black would win a pawn for nothing with 13 … dxe5.

**13   …   h6   14   Bd3   dxe5   15   0–0   b5   16   Qe2   c4
17 Nxe5!**

Because of the strength of the plan associated with White's 12th
and 13th moves, the sub-variation with 9 … g5?! has disappeared
from master praxis. White always gets a very strong attack—and
usually wins. So here.

**17   …   Qb6+   18   Kh1   cxd3   19   Qh5!   Kb8   20   Qxf7+   Kh7
21   d6!   Qxd6   22   Ne4!   Qxe5   23   Nf6+   Qxf6   24   Rxf6   Rg8
25   Rxh6+   Kxh6   26   Qxg8   Nd7   27   Qd5   Ra7   28   Qc6+   Nf6**

**29 Qxc8 Re7 30 h4! Ne4 31 Kh2 gxh5 32 gxh4 Be5+
33 g3! Nxg3 34 Kh3 Bd6 35 Qf8+ Kh7 36 Qxe7+ Bxe7
37 Kxg3 Bf6   38 Rd1 Black resigns**

From a purely strategic standpoint the principle of pawns "capturing toward the center" is always sound. Yet very early in the
opening other factors, such as development, are often of overriding
importance. Consider the Exchange Variation of the Ruy Lopez: 1
e4 e5 2 Nf3 Nf6 3 Bb5 a6 4 Bxf6. According to our principle, 4 ... bxc6
is the correct move. However, after that recapture Black has some
trouble developing and guarding e5, factors that White can exploit
with the active 5 d4!. Therefore, best for Black is the "anticentral"
4 ... dxc6!, since this furthers both the queen's and the queen
bishop's development (5 Nxe5?! is easily parried by 5 ... Qd4!.)

A similar consideration applies to the following line in the Nim-
zovitch Variation of the Sicilian Defense: 1 d4 c5 2 Nf3 Nf6 3 e5 Nd4
4 Nc3 Nxc3. From an immediate central outlook, 5 bxc3 is correct,
but that gives Black the opportunity to annihilate White's e5 outpost with 5 ... d6 and obtain approximate equality. Considerably
stronger for White is the developing 5 dxc3!, since then 5 ... d6 can
be met by 6 exd6!, and whether Black recaptures with 6 ... exd6 or
6 ... Qxd6 7 Qxd6 exd6, his d-pawn will be a serious weakness.

The question of king safety must always be kept in mind when
considering recaptures. For example, after 1 d4 Nf6 2 Bg5 d5 3 Bxf6,
how should Black recapture? If central influence were the only consideration, 3 ... gxf6 would be much the better way. But the h-pawn
is then isolated, and the lack of the g-pawn may make Black's king
somewhat uncomfortable. Therefore, a majority of masters currently prefer the safe, sound, development 3 ... exf6.

The expression "pawn formation" simply means the position of
the pawns as they stand on the board. Often the reference is to a
particular section of the board, be it center, kingside or queenside.
Always remember that an apparently slight change in a pawn formation can have a major fundamental effect.

To illustrate this, let us look at a very common position in the
King's Indian Defense: 1 d4 Nf6 2 c4 g6 3 Nc3 Bg7 4 e4 d6. In eval-
uating this position it is easy to see that White has a considerable
central superiority, due to having three pawns on the fourth rank.
Black, on the other hand, has concentrated on developing his king-

side and has just a bit of central pawn influence. White now has three perfectly logical continuations, each leading to a different central pawn formation:

**DIAGRAM 71**

BLACK

WHITE

*King's Indian Defense, after*
*4 ... d6*

1. *Normal Variation:* 5 Nf3 0–0 6 Be2. Here White says that he is completely satisfied with what he already has in the center.

2. *Sämisch Variation:* 5 f3 0–0 6 Be3. White wants to secure his center and therefore plays 5 f3. The Sämisch is not a sharp attacking variation but a strategic way of trying to ensure that White will remain with a central and spatial advantage.

3. *Four Pawns Attack:* 5 f4 0–0 6 Nf4. White is not satisfied with having "only" three pawns on the fourth rank in the center but wants to have four pawns there! This is a very sharp try at overwhelming Black with early central pawn advances. But note that White has neglected his piece development and his center with four pawns abreast has no safe base of support.

In none of the variations we considered above did White have anything that can be called a structural pawn-formation weakness. Clearly his e-pawn is invulnerable to attack, and therefore Black must look for his central counterplay by challenging White's d-pawn. In the Normal and Sämisch Variations, both ... c5 and ... e5 look logical, but actual experience has shown that the ... e5 advance is the more effective one. In the Four Pawns Attack, White's f-pawn has essentially prevented Black's ... e5, but here ... c5 (e.g., 6 ... c5!) gives excellent counterplay.

There are variations, however—even popular ones—where one side starts off with a fundamental structural weakness. One of the main lines in the Najdorf Variation of the Sicilian Defense goes like this: 1 e4 c5 2 Nf3 d6 3 d4 cxd4 4 Nxd4 Nf6 5 Nc3 a6 6 Be2 e5 7 Nb3.

### DIAGRAM 72

BLACK

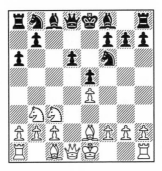

WHITE

*Sicilian Defense, Najdorf*
*Variation, after 7 Nb3*

As a result of 6 ... e5, Black has both chased White's king knight away from the center and gained definite central presence himself.

But there also are two negative features to Black's central advance. First, the d-pawn has become "backward"—i.e., vulnerable to a frontal attack and incapable of a ready advance. As can be seen, the king bishop will have to remain on the inactive e7 square just to keep the d-pawn sufficiently protected. The second negative is that d5 has been permanently weakened, since Black has no remaining pawn that can protect that square.

Because of these negative features, there are many strong players who do not play 6 ... e5 after White's 6 Be2. They prefer either 6 ... e6, transposing into the Scheveningen Variation, where Black has good control of d5, or—despite the 5 ... a6 tempo loss—6 ... g6, transposing into the Dragon Variation. In each instance, the structural weaknesses in Black's pawn formation are considerably less than after 6 ... e5.

Good pawn play requires that we don't voluntarily create weak pawns. Weak pawns are those that are isolated, doubled or backward. As a matter of principle, these should be avoided—unless something valuable is gained in return.

An "isolated" pawn is one by itself; i.e., with no pawn on either of the adjoining files. A characteristic situation results from the following line of the Tarrasch Variation of the French Defense: 1 e4 e6 2 d4 d5 3 Nd2 c5 4 exd5 exd5 5 Bb5+ Nc6 6 Ngf6 Bd6 7 dxc5 Bxc5 8 0–0 Ne7 9 Nb3 Bd6.

### DIAGRAM 73

BLACK

WHITE

*French Defense, Tarrasch
Variation, after 9 ... Bd6*

It is easy to see that Black's d-pawn is fundamentally weak, since there is no other pawn that can support it. In this case Black hopes that the central squares covered by the d-pawn, coupled with the generally free and harmonious development of the minor pieces, will be sufficient compensation for the pawn's inherent weakness.

"Doubled pawns" need not be inherently weak, apart from the obvious weakness of *isolated* doubled pawns. Doubled pawns as part of a pawn cluster may be perfectly satisfactory for defensive purposes. Their major problem is lack of potency in the offense. In the first place, as they advance they can easily leave large gaps in their former territory. Second, there is the problem of not being able to create a passed pawn from certain pawn–majority formations containing doubled pawns.

A formerly much–played line in the Exchange Variation of the Ruy Lopez opens this way: 1 e4 e5 2 Nf3 Nc6 3 Bb5 a6 4 Bxc6 dxc6 5 d4 exd4 6 Qxd4 Qxd4 7 Nxd4.

### DIAGRAM 74

BLACK

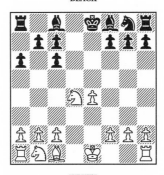

WHITE

*Ruy Lopez, Exchange*
*Variation, after 7 Nxd4*

Though the game has just begun, the characteristic pawn formations are already established. On the kingside, White has a four-vs.-three pawn majority, and it is a "mobile" majority, meaning that White—if he wishes—can create a passed pawn there. On the queenside, Black has a four-vs.-three pawn majority, but Black's majority is a static one. It's fine for defensive purposes, but not of much use for offense. If White plays his queenside pawns correctly, there is no way that Black can force a passed pawn there. For instance, if the a- and b-pawns are exchanged, what we are left with are two c-pawns for Black and one for White—and offensively Black has gotten nowhere. There is no question that in the position after 7 Nxd4 White has the superior pawn formation. As compensation for this, Black must seek open lines and good development for his pieces, in particular his pair of Bishops.

The "backward" pawn was briefly addressed earlier in this chapter when discussing the line in the Najdorf Variation of the Sicilian Defense resulting after 6 Be2 e5 (Diagram 72). There, Black voluntarily accepted the backward pawn in exchange for increased influence over his d5 and e4 squares. As a general principle, however, backward pawns should be avoided because not only are they potentially vulnerable to frontal attack, they are also immobile.

Look at the following schematic diagram of queenside pawns.

**DIAGRAM 75**

BLACK

WHITE

*Schematic diagram of
queenside pawns*

White has a two-vs.-one queenside pawn majority, but how to mobilize it? Wrong is 1 a4?, because this immediately fixes White's b-pawn as backward, since it cannot safely advance to b4. Equally wrong is 1 a3? since after 1 ... a4! White b-pawn is again backward and incapable of advancing. In each of these two cases, Black's single pawn is able to contain two White pawns. The correct way to mobilize the queenside pawns is 1 b3 followed by 2 a3! and 3 b4. Then White is assured of what he wants: creation of a passed pawn from his normal pawn majority.

The pawn weaknesses discussed so far—isolated, doubled and backward—are the most important *structural* weaknesses. What is also important to understand is the concept of *dynamic* pawn weaknesses.

As a pawn advances from its starting position it becomes more vulnerable to attack by enemy pawns and pieces. Of course, most of the time this is nothing to worry about. However, pawn advances in the vicinity of one's own king must always be handled with extreme care. If a direct attack against the king is anticipated, then it is better not to touch the pawns in front of the king at all.

Typical examples of the right and wrong ways are shown arising from the following line of the Scheveningen Variation of the Sicilian Defense: 1 e4 c5 2 Nf3 e6 3 d4 cxd4 4 Nxd4 Nf6 5 Nc3 d6 6 Bc4 Be7 7 Bb3 0–0 8 Be3 Na6 9 f3 Nc5 10 Qd2 a6 11 g4.

**DIAGRAM 76**

BLACK

WHITE

*Sicilian Defense,*
*Scheveningen Variation, after*
*11 g4*

Without question, White has started a direct attack against Black's castled king position. Further, it can be anticipated that White himself will *not* castle on the kingside (more likely on the queenside). White's immediate plan is to dislodge Black's well-placed king knight with 12 g5. What—if anything—should Black do about this threat? Two approaches are plausible.

A) *Wrong is:* 11 ... h6?, since after 12 h4! followed by 13 g5, not only will Black's knight be chased away anyway, but, even more important, the advance of Black's h-pawn means that White will be able to force open a line against Black's king.

B) *The right way* is to leave the kingside alone and to get ready for counterplay on the queenside. Logical, therefore, is 11 ... Qc7! 12 g5 Nfd7 13 h4 b5!. The position remains very double-edged, of course, but extensive master practice has shown that Black's chances are in no way inferior to White's.

PRAISE FOR

## SONGBIRD

'I loved the story of Jamila and the resilience
and bravery of her family. Jamila is a wonderful
character, full of courage and heart, who children
will relate to and learn from.'

SALLY RIPPIN

'A beautiful story full of hope, heartache and love.'

ZANA FRAILLON

'Jamila is a wonderful character and I really loved
*Songbird*...It's a beautiful, hopeful story about digging
deep and helping those around you...a super-great read.'

FIONA HARDY

'A fun, tender and uplifting portrait of a young
Muslim girl's struggle to belong.'

*AEU MAGAZINE*

'An inspiring story...Reading *Songbird* together is a
great way to start conversations with your children
about topical issues, refugees, and to help create
understanding around differences in culture and family.'

*BETTER READING*

'A gentle story about starting over, making friends
and finding a place in the world.'

*MAGPIES*

Ingrid Laguna lives in Melbourne and has
worked with new migrant and refugee children
for many years. *Sunflower* is her second book for
children. It is a companion novel to *Songbird*.

# SUNFLOWER

## INGRID LAGUNA

TEXT PUBLISHING MELBOURNE AUSTRALIA

The Text Publishing Company acknowledges the Traditional Owners of the country on which we work, the Wurundjeri people of the Kulin Nation, and pays respect to their Elders past and present.

textpublishing.com.au

The Text Publishing Company
Wurundjeri Country, Level 6, Royal Bank Chambers, 287 Collins Street, Melbourne, Victoria 3000 Australia

Published by The Text Publishing Company, 2020
Reprinted 2021

Book design by Imogen Stubbs
Cover and internal illustrations by Amy Grimes
Typeset by J&M Typesetting

Printed and bound in Australia by Griffin Press, part of Ovato, an accredited ISO/NZS 14001:2004 Environmental Management System printer.

ISBN: 9781922268754 (paperback)
ISBN: 9781925923308 (ebook)

A catalogue record for this book is available from the National Library of Australia.

This book is printed on paper certified against the Forest Stewardship Council® Standards. Griffin Press holds FSC chain-of-custody certification SGSHK-COC-005088. FSC promotes environmentally responsible, socially beneficial and economically viable management of the world's forests.

The characters and their adventures in this story were inspired by my students who have come to Australia as refugees and started new lives here. This book is for them.

Jamila pressed her hands against the sun-hot glass of the kitchen window. A fan blew warm air around the flat she shared with her mama, baba and little brother Amir. Jamila spun around when the doorbell rang. 'Eva's here!' she said, and ran for the door.

Jamila's mama sat at the kitchen table beside her English tutor, Alina. They kept on with the English lesson. 'Not *runned*,' Alina said to Mama. 'Ran.'

'Ran,' said Mama.

'Good,' said Alina. 'Today I run, yesterday I ran.'

'Mama walks,' said Jamila, bringing Eva into the kitchen.

'*Kun hadiana*, Jamila,' said Mama in Arabic. Be quiet. She greeted Eva with a kiss on the cheek. Jamila felt bad for making jokes. She knew how hard it was to learn English. She knew it made your head hurt and your eyes want to close. And she was glad Mama's English was getting better.

Eva had brought some lemons, which Jamila and Eva were planning to make into a lemon and pistachio cake. 'Jamila and Eva cook,' said Jamila, digging around in the cupboard for flour. She was not in a quiet mood.

Jamila cut the lemons and squeezed out the juice while Eva measured flour, vanilla and sugar into a bowl. Jamila splashed in the lemon juice, milk and a handful of pistachios. She lifted her chin to sing while she stirred the ingredients together.

She could take her voice up high or down low, she could make it sad or rough or let the words out softly. Cake mixture slapped up over the edges of the bowl as she sang.

While Eva added melted butter to icing sugar, she sang with Jamila. She joined in and dropped out with harmonies. She left silences and she filled them up.

Jamila stuck a finger into the mixture and tasted it. *'Ladhidh,'* she said. Delicious.

Jamila and Eva took the cake to Galleon Park. They sat with their backs against the trunk of the banksia tree by the bridge. A magpie landed near Eva. Eva put some cake on her palm and held it out. The bird hopped closer. Jamila had seen birds come to Eva before. The magpie pecked the cake from Eva's hand and then flew up and away.

'Birds aren't scared of you,' said Jamila. 'You're quiet like the sky at night.'

'You're buzzy,' said Eva. 'Like you might start singing at any time.'

Jamila laughed. 'That's true!' she said. 'La-la-la-laaa!'

Birds startled in the trees and Eva laughed.

When they'd finished eating, Jamila and Eva stood on the bridge and made wishes on pebbles they dropped into the water below. Jamila wished for the same thing she always wished for: that Mina, her best friend in Iraq, was safe. She crossed her fingers to make the wish stronger.

Then Eva began to sing, and after a moment, Jamila joined in. Jamila felt the melody lift and shift and hover when she and Eva sang in harmony. She was so happy to have a friend like Eva to sing with.

When Jamila arrived home from the park, she was surprised to see Baba hovering in the doorway. 'I have news,' he said.

'What news?' said Jamila. 'Something bad?'

'Something good,' said Baba. His eyes were bright. 'Mina's coming to Australia. Mina and her mama and baba. Their visas have been approved.'

Jamila had been waiting for this day, waiting and hoping and praying. She knew from the TV news that there was still trouble in Iraq. A lot of trouble. Jamila had left Iraq six months ago, but she still missed Mina every day.

'She's really coming?' said Jamila.

'They're flying into Melbourne on Wednesday,' said Baba.

'*Wednesday*?' said Jamila. Excitement fizzed inside her.

'Wednesday,' said Baba.

There had been times when Jamila had thought she would never see Mina again. She had lain awake at night worrying about Mina and imagining the worst. Now Mina had a visa and soon she would be on a plane.

Jamila had made a whole new life since leaving Iraq. She had friends at school and her English was much better. She sang in the school choir and didn't worry when people sometimes looked at her strangely for wearing a headscarf. She wondered if Mina would like Australia. Would she come to school with Jamila? Would she get along with Eva?

Mina had sewn a purse from fox-print fabric for Jamila when they were in Baghdad together. Jamila picked up the purse and read the Arabic word Mina had stitched onto the front. It was the nickname Mina had given Jamila years earlier.

*Mutraba.*

Songbird.

2

Jamila couldn't wait to speak Arabic with Mina. She couldn't wait to tell her everything about life here in Australia, her new home.

Today was a school day. Jamila packed extra *klecha*, cardamom and date biscuits, to share with Eva. She hoped Eva might bring her a blueberry muffin or some cheesy doritos. Jamila and Eva spent all their time at school together. They sat next to each other in class and sang side by side in the school choir. At recess and lunch time they spread their food out on the grass between them to share. Jamila brought dolma, semolina cake and *biryani*, spicy rice with chicken. Eva had egg sandwiches, oranges and muffins. Jamila couldn't wait for Mina to meet Eva.

Jamila took the bus to school, past the shop that sold caramello koalas, the bakery where she and Mama bought cinnamon donuts, and the train station dotted with waiting people. She would walk these streets with Mina soon. She would share Australian sweets with her, milky ways and wagon wheels, and take her on the train to the city.

Eva was waiting at the school gate when Jamila arrived. She waved to Jamila and the birthmark across her cheek changed shape a little as she smiled.

'I have *klecha*,' said Jamila, lifting her schoolbag into the air. 'Biscuits.'

'Cheese stringers,' said Eva, pointing to her own bag. 'String made of cheese!'

Jamila thought of *geymar*, the thickened cream

Mina's mama used to lather onto bread with date syrup for Jamila and Mina. It was hard to believe that Mina's mama and baba would be in Australia soon too. Mina's parents were like an aunt and uncle to Jamila.

'Guess what?' said Jamila, and then she went on before Eva could speak. 'Mina and her family will be here in just three more sleeps!'

Jamila saw a shadow of worry cross Eva's face. 'Really?' she said.

'You will like her!' said Jamila. 'She calls me *Mutraba*, which means a girl who is always singing. Or Songbird. My nickname.'

'I know,' said Eva. 'You've told me a hundred times.' Eva looked away as she leant down to pick up her bag.

Looking at Eva, Jamila realised that she wasn't as happy as Jamila was about Mina's arrival. At school, Jamila was Eva's best friend, and Eva was Jamila's. What would happen when Mina came?

*

When Jamila and Eva arrived at their classroom, Miss Sarah was writing on the whiteboard. 'Morning!' she said. She wore a checked shirt with sleeves rolled up to her elbows. She smelt like buttery fruit toast.

Miss Sarah's dog slept on a cushion next to her desk. The dog's name was Luna and he was white with grey patches fringing his ears. Jamila couldn't wait for Mina to meet Luna. No one loved dogs more than Mina. Jamila and Eva crouched beside Luna and ruffled his fur.

'Luna's a bolognese,' said Miss Sarah, kneeling beside Jamila.

Jamila had tasted spaghetti bolognese at Eva's house. She had scraped her bowl clean and asked for more. She looked at Miss Sarah, confused.

'The breed name is bolognese because it comes from Bologna,' Miss Sarah explained. 'In Italy.'

'In Baghdad,' said Jamila, 'there were stray

dogs roaming the streets. One time I was walking with my friend Mina and we saw a boy holding a stick up in the air, about to hit a puppy that was just standing there, not hurting anyone.'

Eva spread her fingers over her open mouth. Miss Sarah leaned in closer to listen.

'Mina ran over and stood between the boy and the dog,' said Jamila. 'The boy told her to move. But Mina shook her head. The boy said bad words to Mina, but then he walked away.'

'Mina saved the dog?' said Eva.

'Yes,' said Jamila. 'She took him to the animal shelter and called him Sami.'

'Mina sounds brave,' said Eva. 'I've never done anything like that.'

Jamila thought about this. It was true that Mina was brave. But Eva had lots of good qualities too. Eva listened all the way to the end of a story. She didn't interrupt or look away when Jamila talked about the nightmares that rushed into her sleep. She didn't laugh when Jamila said 'drinked' instead of 'drank'. And Eva noticed things. She pointed out the reflection of the sky in a puddle. She found beetles and let them climb onto her palm.

Jamila wanted to tell Eva that when Mina came, all three of them could be best friends. But was it true? Jamila and Mina had grown up together. They were practically sisters. But here in Australia, Eva helped Jamila through each long school day, fixing her sentences and helping her with her spelling. And when they sang together, Eva's harmonies threaded through Jamila's melodies like just-right ingredients in a cake. Eva was Jamila's best friend in Australia. But what did that make Mina? Jamila didn't know.

Today was the day. Mina was on the plane right now. Jamila looked out the window as if she might see an aeroplane emerge from the clouds, delivering her friend to her. She sat on the rug with her baby brother, Amir. She sang to him. She stuck out her tongue and crossed her eyes to make him laugh. She remembered Mina fluttering her eyelashes against Amir's cheeks as he gurgled and clutched at her headscarf.

Jamila got up and went to stand just outside her front door. She imagined seeing her flat through

Mina's eyes, with bricks the colour of rust and paint peeling off the front fence. She could hear people slamming doors in the flats above and beside her own. She could smell their fried sausages and hear their footsteps. Jamila didn't live in a palace. But she was grateful every day that she did not hear gunfire or the echo of bombs. She did not see walls peppered with bullet holes or men with masks covering their faces. Jamila and her family were safe now. And soon Mina would be safe too.

'*Al hamdu li'Allah*,' she whispered. Praise God.

Jamila stepped up to the curb and peered around the corner. Baba was picking up Mina and her family from the airport when he finished work and bringing them to Jamila's house. A distant revving engine might be Baba's car. Jamila couldn't wait to have sleepovers with Mina and talk until midnight. She would take Mina to Galleon Park. She pictured Mina skipping and giggling and drawing her beloved sunflowers with her finger in the air while they walked together.

Finally, Baba's car did turn into Jamila's street. Jamila held her breath. Mina spilled from the car and ran to Jamila, nearly toppling her as they hugged each other tight. When they let go and took a step back, Jamila had to hide her shock. Mina was thin. Her shoulders were poking through her top. Her clothes were frayed. Her eyes were rimmed with dark circles. Her skin was as white as bones.

4

Jamila had dreamt of Mina joining her at school ever since her first days in Australia. She had told Miss Sarah that Mina was an artist who drew sunflowers with bright yellow petals facing up to the sun. She had imagined Mina stroking Luna and telling Miss Sarah about Sami, the puppy she had rescued and raised at the animal shelter in Baghdad.

Now Mina and her family were staying at Jamila's flat until they found a place of their own and Jamila was bursting for Mina to come to school. But each morning, Mina shook her head.

'No,' she said. 'Not today.' And neither her mama, Aziza, nor her baba, Mohamed, said she had to go.

'When you're ready,' said Aziza.

'Just rest, *habibty*,' said Mohamed, as if Mina was broken and needed time to mend.

Jamila could see that Mina was not as strong as she used to be. She reminded Jamila of a skeleton character from a movie she had seen. It had dark, deep sockets for eyes and knobbly shoulders and knees. Jamila could see the lines of Mina's cheeks and jawbone. Even her fingers were thin.

More than anything, it was the look in Mina's eyes that kept surprising Jamila. She knew that the fighting in Iraq was still bad. She could imagine all too well what Mina might have seen or heard. But Jamila had become used to feeling safe in Australia. If Mina came to school, she could make friends and meet Luna.

'Can you believe there is an actual real-life dog

in our classroom?' said Jamila. She unpinned her headscarf and let her hair loose. 'We can sit with Luna whenever we want. Miss Sarah says *dogs are all about love and who doesn't need love?*'

Mina smiled weakly. Jamila wished she had a photo of Luna to show her, with his eyes peeking through his frizzy fringe. Maybe then Mina would want to come to school.

Jamila talked about her friends. 'Georgia knows facts,' she said. 'Like that butterflies can taste with their feet. And wild dolphins call each other by name.' Jamila made dolphin noises to make Mina laugh, but Mina's eyes were blank. She was looking at Jamila, but Jamila could tell her mind was elsewhere.

Jamila thought back to her first weeks in Australia. She remembered fear tingling in the palms of her hands at shop counters. She remembered her heart thumping when she was just sitting at her desk in the classroom. Even once you were safe, the worry didn't go away. Jamila knew that. But it was still hard for her to understand why Mina didn't want to come to school.

'You'll like Alice and Winnie,' said Jamila. 'We play handball together. You can play too.'

Mina was holding a small blanket she had brought with her from Baghdad, running her palm over the fabric.

'Are you listening to me?' said Jamila. She used her gentlest voice.

'*Na-em*.' said Mina. Yes.

'Finn's okay,' said Jamila. 'He's just annoying. And Bethany...she wants to know everybody's business. She asks a lot of questions.'

Mina put the blanket under the pillow on her floor-bed. She was sleeping in Jamila's room, while her parents slept on the couch in the living room.

'Did you sleep well last night?' asked Jamila. She had heard Mina tossing and calling out in her sleep.

'*Showyah.*' A bit.

'Did you have bad dreams?' asked Jamila.

In Baghdad, Jamila and Mina had always shared their dreams.

'I dreamt of Sami,' said Mina. She looked out the window into the small square of courtyard.

'You must miss him,' said Jamila.

Mina shook her head as if to flick the memories away. 'Don't you have to go to school?' she said.

'Yes,' said Jamila. And then she added, softly, 'I just want you to be happy here.'

'I know,' said Mina.

It was another six days before Jamila led Mina through the gates for her first day at school. A girl zoomed by on a scooter. A ball flew up and a boy ran past to catch it. Mums and dads talked and jiggled prams. Mina's head swivelled this way and that, in quick, birdlike motions. Jamila was pleased to see Eva waiting at the gates to greet them. Her smile was friendly.

'This is Mina,' said Jamila. She had been looking forward to this moment.

'Hi,' said Eva.

Mina's school dress hung loose, as if it belonged to a bigger girl. She wore her headscarf close around her face. There were bruised patches under her frightened eyes. Jamila felt sad when she looked at Mina.

'Hello,' said Mina, forcing a smile.

A baby cried out and Mina jumped, looking around like she wanted somewhere to hide. Jamila put a hand on Mina's arm. '*Maykhalef*,' she said. It's okay.

Mina's eyes nervously scanned the school buildings. Jamila remembered a time when Mina liked making new friends. She was not smiling now.

'Come and meet Miss Sarah,' said Jamila. 'And Luna, our classroom dog.' She hooked her arm through Mina's. '*Yalla*,' she said. Come on.

Miss Sarah was standing in the doorway.

'This is Mina,' said Jamila.

'Welcome,' said Miss Sarah, thrusting her

palm out to shake Mina's hand. Mina flinched at the sudden movement.

'*Shukraan*,' said Mina quietly. Thank you.

Jamila had learnt that in Australia, kids were supposed to look into the eyes of adults when they spoke to them. Instead, Mina shot anxious glances around the classroom. She looked at the Word Wall. There were words for describing people: *energetic, creative, interesting.* There were words for feelings: *hopeful, stressed, enthusiastic.* Jamila guessed what Mina was thinking. She could not see one word in her own language. Jamila stepped closer to Mina. '*Enta bekher?*' she said. Are you okay?

Mina nodded.

'Hey, Mina,' said Eva, crouching beside Miss Sarah's sleeping dog. 'This is Luna.'

Luna opened his eyes at the sound of his name. Jamila was hopeful. She knew that Mina loved dogs.

But Mina did not crouch beside Luna. She did not light up and coo and stroke Luna's fluffy ears. She stretched her mouth into a smile that Jamila could tell was not real.

'You're allowed to pat him,' said Jamila. '*Yalla.*'

Mina hesitated, then she knelt beside Luna. She held her palm under his chin and looked into his eyes. Luna's tail swished through the air. Jamila searched Mina's face for signs of joy. She only saw sadness.

Jamila thought back to her own first day at this school. She remembered forgetting her English words and feeling like everyone was looking at her. Before she met Eva, Jamila hid behind books or sharpened her pencils until they were down to stumps the size of her little finger.

In class, Mina sat on one side of Jamila and Eva sat on the other. Jamila was glad they were starting the day with art, because it was Mina's favourite subject. Miss Sarah placed a jar of flowers on a desk. Jamila wished there were sunflowers in the vase instead of wilting gerberas. Mina and Jamila had walked along the edge of a sunflower field in Iraq once. The flowers came up to their shoulders and smelt wild and sweet.

Mina's hand trembled as she sketched in silence beside Jamila. She drew perfectly formed petals and leaves.

Before Jamila left Iraq, there had not been even the tiniest of secrets between herself and Mina. Jamila had told Mina when Mama and Baba were fighting. She had called Mina in tears when Baba had been arrested for writing news articles about the fighting in Iraq. And Mina had told Jamila when she found a kitten under her house, even before she told her own mama.

Now it seemed that Mina's life in Iraq since Jamila had left was a dark thing, a secret they didn't share. Mina drew the jar holding the flowers. Her thin chest rose and fell in shallow breaths and Jamila felt her heart crack.

Jamila wanted to talk to Eva about Mina, but she couldn't. She didn't want Mina to feel left out. She was sitting between her two best friends but she couldn't really talk to either of them.

When Jamila led Mina out into the playground, she was glad Eva tagged along.

'We have the best hiding spot,' said Jamila, pointing to a eucalyptus tree that rose high above the fence line in a far corner of the yard. '*Yalla*, Mina.'

Nearby, a man in overalls was cutting branches from bushes with giant, scissor-like clippers.

'Who's that?' said Mina, stopping suddenly.

'The gardener,' said Jamila, stopping too.

Mina blinked every time the blades clapped

together. *Snap. Snap. Snap.*

'Let's wait until he goes,' said Mina.

'You don't have to worry,' said Jamila.

In Baghdad, before Jamila came to Australia, she felt the same way Mina did. When there was trouble in their village, they were scared together. But Jamila had been in Australia for many months now.

'The gardener is not going to hurt us,' said Jamila. 'I promise.' She took Mina's hand and led her to the tree. Eva and Jamila had been sharing this shady spot at break times ever since they became friends. They had lined it with pebbles and sticks from around the playground.

'We share our lunches,' said Jamila, unpacking *biryani*, flatbread, and homemade red pepper dip. Eva laid out a sandwich cut into quarters, a muesli bar and an apple. Mina took the lid off her lunch box.

'Mina brought *margat bamya*,' said Jamila,

leaning towards the tub and inhaling deeply. 'Her mama made it for our dinner last night. You have to taste some, Eva. It has lamb and okra and spicy tomatoes.'

'What's okra?' asked Eva.

Mina held out her fork with a small green vegetable on it. 'Okra,' said Mina. 'Try it.' She glanced warily at the gardener.

Eva ate the okra. 'Strange,' she said. She offered Mina a square of her sandwich, but Mina shook her head. 'No…thank you.'

Jamila wanted to tell Eva that Mina had never eaten the fluffy white squares of bread that kids in Australia sometimes ate. She wanted to say, she's not used to the food here, but she will like your food. She will like *you*.

Eva offered Mina her muesli bar. 'It's got choc chips in it,' she said.

Jamila knew that Eva loved muesli bars. She wondered if she would offer her favourite food to an almost-stranger to make her feel better. Jamila wanted to thank Eva for being there. She wanted to tell her she was sorry that Mina wasn't much fun at the moment.

Jamila's class spent the afternoon learning about Australian animals that were in danger of becoming extinct. They learnt that rock wallabies were in trouble because of foxes and wild cats. They worked in pairs and then they watched a documentary. When Miss Sarah asked questions at the end of the session, Jamila heard Mina mutter answers quietly to herself. Good answers.

Jamila wanted her classmates to know that her friend from Iraq was clever. She imagined taking Mina's hand and pulling it into the air for her. She could take Mina's chin between her finger and thumb and open her mouth to let the answers out. But she knew that Mina was scared. Everything was new for her. She wasn't ready to speak in front of the whole class. Jamila clasped her hands together under the desk and kept her mouth shut. Be patient, she told herself. Give her time.

When the final bell rang, Jamila and Mina walked to the bus stop. Kids chatted and called out to one another as they headed home. But the silence between the two girls was thick like *harees* porridge. Jamila understood that Mina needed time to adjust. She had been living with the constant threat of danger in Iraq. But Jamila was not patient. And this made her cross with herself for expecting too much from her friend.

Jamila also missed Eva. She missed having just one best friend. The thought of trying to juggle her two friendships again the next day made Jamila feel tired all over. The walk to the bus stop felt suddenly far too long.

7

Jamila picked up Mina's lace-trimmed headscarf. It smelt like *halawa*, the milk sweets that Mina loved to eat. Mina's parents had found a place for their family to live. Now Jamila was helping Mina to pack her things back into her suitcase.

'I remember when you bought this scarf at the night market in Najaf,' said Jamila.

'Your baba bought one the same for you,' said Mina. 'Do you still have it?'

Jamila remembered packing to leave her home in Baghdad. The task had been impossible. Was

Australia hot or cold? Should she bring the song book her Uncle Elias had given her? And what about the necklace her cousin had made? It had Jamila's name curved into a copper chain. She had packed the song book, put the chain around her neck and squashed whatever clothes she could fit into her suitcase.

'I left the scarf in Iraq,' said Jamila. 'I wanted to bring everything, but I couldn't. I filled my suitcase and then I walked around the house touching all the things we had to leave behind.'

Mina's hair was loose over her shoulders and her dark, pretty eyes were focused and serious. 'I wanted to bring everything too,' she said. 'I piled my clothes and scarves onto my bed. And my sewing box and photos and—' Mina abandoned her sentence, the words catching in her throat.

Jamila put a hand on Mina's arm. 'It's hard,' she said softly.

A breeze blew in the open window and Mina sighed.

'We're just kids,' said Jamila. 'We're supposed to be running around and having fun.' She wanted to distract Mina from sad thoughts. 'It's good we can still walk to the park from your new house.' When Mina drew trees and ducks at the park, she whistled on the walk home afterwards.

'And we can still go to school together,' Jamila added, hopeful her school life with Mina and Eva would soon get easier.

'*Na-em*,' said Mina, squeezing out a smile. Yes.

Jamila and Mina could hear their parents' voices coming from the kitchen. Jamila liked hearing them all speak Arabic together, like they used to do at home in Iraq. Home is the language of your first words and the smell of cardamom, cloves and paprika, she thought.

'Let's go for a walk,' said Jamila.

'Where?' said Mina. 'Walk where?'

'To the shop,' said Jamila. 'Let's buy milky ways.'

Mina stood beside her half-packed bag. 'I don't even know what that is,' she said. She rubbed her eyes with her fists. She was tired beyond sleep. Jamila could tell from the web of red lines running out from her pupils and the droop of her shoulders.

'It will be okay,' said Jamila.

'*Le namshi*,' said Mina. Let's walk.

Jamila and Mina walked past the apartment block with big iron gates and the crumbling house on the corner with the sleeping ginger cat stretched across its front door.

'When we left our house,' said Mina, 'I picked up my suitcase and followed Mama out the door. I said to myself—*Mina, don't look back*. But the house was calling me. I didn't look back, Jamila. And now, I want to see my house again.'

Jamila knew how Mina felt. Waves of home-sickness sometimes washed over her when she didn't know they were coming. Once she had seen Zaid, a boy from school in Baghdad. She had even called his name, excited to see a familiar face from her old life. The boy turned to her, but it was not Zaid. That afternoon, Jamila had climbed into Amir's cot and curled up next to him while he slept. She ached to be home in Kadhimiya, Baghdad.

When Jamila and Mina reached the shop, Jamila bought two milky way chocolate bars. Mina took a bite and scrunched up her nose.

'You don't like it?' said Jamila. 'Really?'

Mina shook her head.

'That's okay,' said Jamila, trying not to show her disappointment.

Eva had given Jamila her first milky way. Eva said they were creamy and just-right. Jamila agreed.

8

Jamila sat beside Mina at the kitchen table that afternoon to help her with her homework. Mina had to write a story in one hundred words that began with the line:

*The boy's hands shook as he took the letter from the envelope.*

Mina wrote:

*The boy scared. What does the letter say? The man find his sister?*

'It's good,' said Jamila. 'Keep going.' Jamila had finished her own story in class.

Mina placed the tip of the pen against her palm and drew a swirl that started small and grew outwards. Jamila saw that she was pressing the pen tip hard against her skin. The skin creased and whitened where she pushed on it.

'Stop!' said Jamila. 'You're hurting yourself.' Jamila twisted the pen from Mina's grip. She pulled Mina's writing book over.

'How about...*The boy had not seen his sister for so long*,' she said.

'Okay,' said Mina. She dropped her head to one side as though it was too heavy to hold up.

Jamila wrote the first few words and then returned the pen and book to Mina. 'You're good at writing stories,' she said. Jamila wondered if she should tell Mama about Mina pressing the sharp point of the pen against her skin. It frightened Jamila.

'I'm not good at writing stories in English,' said Mina.

'It gets easier,' said Jamila. 'With practice, writing in English gets easier.'

Mina wrote slowly, looping and joining the letters. Her letters were wobbly and unevenly sloped. Jamila remembered her own struggle with writing when she first came to Australia.

Mina put down her pen. 'Enough,' she said.

Jamila remembered Mina writing whole pages without looking up at school in Baghdad.

'I'm tired,' said Mina. 'I think I might go back to bed.'

'I guess that's okay,' said Jamila, even though it wasn't. Jamila's mama had stayed in her bed when she was missing Baba, before he came to Australia. Jamila knew that staying in bed just led to more staying in bed. It made your feelings go down instead of up.

Jamila wished she could talk to Eva. She wished she could bake and sing and go to the park with her. An uncomfortable thought nagged at

Jamila: her life had been easier before Mina came. The thought made her feel like a bad friend.

'Do you want to hear a song I wrote?' said Jamila. Singing usually made her feel better.

'Of course,' said Mina. 'I will sleep later.' Her smile was like a small gift and Jamila was grateful. She took out her song book and began to sing. Mina picked up her drawing paper and started to draw. It was like the old days. Maybe everything would be okay.

*9*

Jamila's friends, Alice and Winnie, were opposites. Alice had a round face and was always trying out different hairstyles. One day she wore lots of tiny plaits and another time she skipped through the school gates with a crooked, short fringe. She wore penguin earrings and stripy socks. She whistled a lot. Winnie had a pointy chin and ignored her permanently scruffy hair. She had been tap-dancing since she was five. No earrings. Plain socks.

'Jamila!' called Alice. She had a side ponytail tied with an orange pipe cleaner. 'Do you want to come and play handball?'

'Yes!' said Jamila. She turned to Mina and Eva. 'Come on. We can all have a turn.'

'But I don't know how,' said Mina. 'I can't—'

'Just watch first, Mina,' said Jamila. 'Then we'll swap when you're ready. Okay?' Sometimes Jamila felt a bit like Mina's babysitter. It was not a good feeling.

'Okay,' said Mina.

'You're not allowed to let the ball hit the line,' said Alice, 'or let it bounce more than once in your own square.'

Lines marking out squares were drawn in chalk on the concrete between the classroom blocks.

Jamila and Eva took their positions and Jamila re-pinned her hijab. She remembered throwing a ball with Baba and Uncle Elias and Mina in Baghdad. She remembered Mina laughing.

Winnie bounced the ball down in front of Jamila. It flew up and Jamila caught it. She bounced it to Winnie who bounced it to Eva. They played on until beads of sweat appeared on Jamila's forehead. Mina had been watching with folded arms.

'Do you want a turn?' asked Jamila.

Mina chewed her lip. Jamila knew Mina was good at throwing and catching. 'You'll like it,' she said.

'Okay,' said Mina, stepping gingerly into Jamila's square.

Alice bounced the ball in front of Mina. Mina caught it. She looked pleased. Jamila watched from the sideline like the stakes were high. Her heart thumped as if she was in the square with Mina.

'Don't hold onto it,' said Alice. 'Keep it moving.'

Mina bounced the ball to Alice and Alice bounced it to Winnie. When Winnie smacked it down in front of Mina, Mina's hands fumbled and Jamila gasped. But Mina caught the ball and then played on. Soon she turned to Jamila. 'Your turn,' she said. There was a new confidence about her and it made Jamila feel lighter.

Jamila hurled the ball down in Alice's square. She kept her hands up and eyes on the ball and the game played on. *Bounce. Bounce. Bounce.*

When Jamila next turned to look at Mina, she saw she was crying, shaking and hiccupping. Bethany had a hand on her shoulder. Jamila tossed the ball to Winnie and rushed over.

'What happened?' said Jamila.

'We were just talking,' said Bethany. 'I said… I just asked—'

'What?' said Jamila. 'You asked what?'

'I asked why she left Iraq. She started to tell me and then—'

'You and your questions,' said Jamila. She huffed air out her nose. 'You should think first.'

Maybe Mina tried to tell Bethany about the long night she spent lying flat under her bed waiting for gunfire to pass. Maybe she tried to describe the sound of rock and metal pummelling buildings.

Jamila led Mina to a quiet corner of the library. She remembered Mina around the time she found Sami. If someone had asked her a question she did not want to answer, she would have jutted her chin and said, 'Who are you to ask me this?' Now she sat shakily beside Jamila. Jamila wished bad memories could be taken away by a surgeon, the way shrapnel had been removed from her cousin's leg.

After school, Jamila and Eva went to the hall for choir. Mina was not sure how to take the bus home by herself, so she came along too. She sat to the side of the room, but Jamila could feel her there. She stopped herself from laughing with Eva. She had to hold a giggle in her mouth and the more she held it in the more the giggle wanted to come out.

The giggle went away when Jamila looked at

Mina. Mina wasn't watching Jamila and Eva. Mina was thinking. There were creases between her brows and one knee jigged up and down. Jamila wanted to wrap her in muslin and take her home. She wanted to say to Mina's mama, Aziza, *Mina is not ready for any of this.* But what could Aziza do?

10

Eva knew where to find things in Jamila's kitchen without thinking. She pulled out a mixing bowl, flour, sugar and eggs. Jamila lined up oranges and squeezed out the juice. 'I call this recipe orange and sour cream cake,' she said. 'It's an experiment.'

It was a warm Saturday morning. Mina was searching around in the cupboard.

'What are you looking for?' said Jamila.

'A measuring cup,' said Mina. She crouched to look under the kitchen bench.

'Eva knows where it is,' said Jamila. 'How

about you stir?'

'Oh,' said Mina. *'Hasannon.'* Okay.

Jamila nudged Mina and whispered, 'English.' Mina rolled her eyes.

When Mina pulled out the cutlery drawer, she bumped Jamila and orange juice spilled over the benchtop.

'Woah!' exclaimed Jamila.

Mina mopped up the juice. *'Asif,'* she said. 'Sorry.'

'It's okay,' said Jamila.

'Here,' said Eva, handing Mina a wooden spoon.

Jamila and Eva moved in sync with each other, taking turns to add ingredients to the bowl while Mina stirred. They sang a song Mina had not heard before and laughed at the same time during the chorus. Jamila tried to think of a song that Mina and Eva might both know but nothing came to her mind.

*

When the cake was ready, Jamila suggested they go to Galleon Park. The footpath was not wide enough for the three of them, so Jamila walked behind. She noticed the polite distance Eva and Mina kept between them, but at least they were talking. At the park, they all sat under the banksia tree and let cake crumbs fall on the picnic blanket as they ate.

'Hey, Mina,' said Jamila. 'Remember Zamir? The funny man who sold *hummus bi tahina* at the Al Shorja market?'

'Yes,' said Mina. 'He was crazy.'

'And remember the time we ate so much we groaned all the way home?' said Jamila.

Mina smiled. 'Oh, but it was delicious!'

Jamila turned to Eva. '*Hummus bi tahina* has whole chickpeas with the tahini. It is nutty and sticky and yum.'

'Can you make it?' asked Eva.

'Mina's mama makes it the best,' said Jamila.

'Remember the spices at the market?' said Mina. 'In little mountains...red, yellow and brown.' Her gaze ran over the treetops and buildings in the distance. 'I miss that market.'

'Me too,' said Jamila. She was glad Mina was remembering good things about Iraq.

When they finished the cake, Jamila stood and pointed to the bridge. 'Race you!' she said and took off. Eva and Mina followed. When they got there, they leant over the railing and Jamila and Eva began to sing a song from choir. Mina clapped when the song finished, but soon after she said she had a headache and asked Jamila to take her home.

Jamila didn't want to leave Eva.

'Go,' said Eva, feeling around in her bag. 'I'm fine. I want to read.' She took out a book and flicked her hand in the air. 'Really.'

Mina stood with her fingers pressed to her forehead.

'Okay,' said Jamila. 'See you soon.'

'Yep,' said Eva.

'I'm sorry,' said Mina as they left the park. 'Will Eva be okay?'

Jamila thought for a moment. 'She's reading a book she loves,' she said. 'I think she'll be alright.'

A cat crossed the footpath and disappeared under a fence. Mina talked about the kitten she had found in Baghdad. Jamila and Mina had hidden the kitten in Mina's bedroom for two days. They knew Mohamed would not let Mina keep it. Jamila remembered how close their friendship used to be.

But was Jamila a bad friend for leaving Eva at the park? She remembered putting on a concert with Eva for her family and Eva's Aunt Marisa, before Mina came to Australia. They had lined up chairs and handed out tickets. Amir stood between Jamila and Eva, holding their hands. When they bowed, he tipped his body forward to bow too. The girls stopped him from falling just in time and the audience laughed and clapped.

Jamila pictured Eva alone at the park and sighed. She couldn't let Mina walk home by herself, but she didn't like leaving Eva either. Jamila was usually good at fixing problems. But here she was being pulled in two directions at once when there was only one of her.

11

The school choir leader, Ms Carrington, wore polished shoes and carried song sheets in a brief-case. She held herself straight-backed like a dancer and kept her feelings to herself. Even when Lan bumped a table and Ms Carrington's favourite teacup smashed on the floor she did not snap. She mopped up the tea and kept on with the session.

But today Ms Carrington's eyes were blood-shot. 'Please sit,' she said. Jamila and Eva glanced at one another. Ms Carrington never let them sit.

'I have some news,' said Ms Carrington. Her

voice sounded shaky. 'It's not good news, I'm afraid.'

Jamila loved Ms Carrington almost as much as she loved choir itself. Ms Carrington took singing seriously. She treated choir as though it was more important than long division or geography or the life cycle of plants. Jamila noticed that today Ms Carrington had missed a buttonhole on her shirt so that her collar sat slightly higher on one side.

Jamila had a bad feeling.

Ms Carrington opened her mouth as if to speak, but then closed it again. She sat down on the piano stool and then stood back up. 'I need to let you know that for now,' she said, 'this choir can't…' She twisted her hands together. The school receptionist appeared in the doorway. She gave Ms Carrington a small nod, as if to say *go on*. 'I'm moving to Sydney,' said Ms Carrington. 'I have to. My brother is…not well.' There were worry lines around her eyes. 'Not well at all.' She looked at the choir before her. Her gaze met Jamila's. 'I'm sorry, but there will be no more choir.'

Choir day was Jamila's favourite day of the week.

No more choir meant no more favourite day.

Jamila still struggled to write sentences with big words at school, or to give speaking presentations. She was still better at Arabic than she was at English. But Jamila could sing better than anyone else in the school.

Jamila looked at Eva. Eva looked back, her eyes big and round.

Ms Carrington said she was sorry again and then dropped her folder. She bent to pick it up and when she stood, Jamila saw her eyes were glassy with tears. 'This choir has been...' She looked around for words. 'Just...keep singing.' She turned and left the hall, leaving the school receptionist to finish up the session.

No more choir.

'Ms Carrington was almost crying,' Jamila said to Eva. 'And now she's leaving.'

'I *love* choir,' said Eva. 'I would rather give up art or Italian or—'

'I would rather give up *school*,' said Jamila.

Jamila and Eva met up with Mina, who was waiting for them at the school gates. Her school bag sagged from one narrow shoulder as if it might pull her down onto the gravel with its weight. Jamila told her Ms Carrington's news.

'Can't someone else run the choir?' said Mina. 'Like Miss Sarah?'

'Only if Ziggy can come,' said Jamila. 'Her horse!'

'And Luna,' added Eva.

'And some fish from her fishpond,' said Mina.

They laughed until they remembered the not-good news.

\*

Sitting on the bus beside Mina, Jamila's shoulders slumped. Her mouth could not smile, even for the friendly bus driver. Without choir, what did Jamila have to look forward to? Mina was still quiet and jittery. And her friendship with Eva was changing. It had sticky moments when Jamila had to leave Eva to be with Mina.

Mina got off at her stop and the bus moved on. It rumbled along streets Jamila knew, but now the houses and shops looked different, as if all the colour had drained away.

At home, Jamila caught her reflection in the bathroom mirror as she washed her hands. She turned on the tap so hard that water splashed onto her top and she didn't care. She sang quietly:

*Just when I have found a reason*
*Just when I can see the sun*

Jamila stood up straight. She kept singing, making

up the words on the spot.

*Change has found its way to me*
*And now again I'm on the run*

An idea was settling over Jamila. She knew lots of songs. And she could write new ones. Eva knew how to sing harmonies, high parts and low ones. They could run their *own* choir.

Jamila rang Mina first.

'Your own choir?' said Mina. 'You and Eva? But how?' Mina sounded doubtful.

'I don't know exactly,' said Jamila. She wanted to hang up and call Eva. Eva shared Jamila's passion for singing. Eva would know what to say. 'I have to go,' she said. 'Mama's calling me.' A lie.

Jamila rang Eva. Eva said, 'Yes. Yes. Yes.'

When they hung up, Jamila took out her song book. She was bursting with ideas waiting to spill out into the shapes of songs. She couldn't wait to tell Baba. He would run his fingers through his beard and nod his head. Baba liked it when Jamila thought for herself and made brave choices. His eyes said, *That's my Jamila.*

When Jamila saw Eva the next morning, she tilted her head back and sang, 'Laaa…'

Eva joined her, singing a note that started lower than Jamila's and then slid up to sit above it.

'Impressive, girls,' said Miss Sarah, passing by.

Our own choir, thought Jamila. Mine and Eva's. She turned to Mina. 'Will you help us make posters for the choir?' she said. She didn't want Mina to feel left out. Mina didn't answer straight away. Jamila felt annoyed. She hadn't asked Mina to name the planets in alphabetical order or to list eight different types of gas. She was just trying to include her.

'Okay,' said Mina.

'Great,' said Jamila, hoping she sounded better than she felt.

They made posters:

Come and join
Jamila and Eva's

## Grade 6 Choir

Friday lunch time
In the shelter shed

Snacks and songs provided

'I've checked with Mrs Ward,' said Miss Sarah. 'You can put the posters up around the school.'

The idea of announcing the choir to the whole school made Jamila dizzy with excitement. When she pinned a poster to the library noticeboard, the librarian's expression became dreamy. 'I used to be in a choir,' she said.

Beza slid two fingers down the poster. 'Did you get permission to put these up?' she asked.

'Yes,' said Jamila. She knew to keep her answer as short as possible. Beza had said not-nice things to Jamila in the past. She had told her that singing was *haram*, forbidden for Muslim girls. She had a way of making problems when you didn't see them coming.

While Jamila and Eva wrapped a poster around a playground pole, Finn asked, 'What sort of snacks?'

'Baba ghanoush and pita bread,' said Jamila.

'Baba what?' said Finn, as if he'd sucked on a lemon. Jamila rolled her eyes.

'Dips and bread,' said Eva.

'And *klecha*,' said Mina.

'Sounds weird,' said Finn.

'It's not all about the snacks,' said Jamila.

'It is for me,' said Finn.

When Miss Sarah let Jamila write about choir in a corner of the whiteboard, Georgia said, 'Great! Friday lunch time.' Jamila could have hugged her. She pictured herself and Eva standing in front of all the kids from Ms Carrington's choir. Maybe the heat would come into the shed or the wind would blow, but no one would notice because they would be too busy singing.

12

Jamila and Eva ran straight to the shelter shed when the lunch bell rang on Friday. They watched kids spilling out of classroom buildings, skipping or walking to the north oval, the south oval or the playground.

Jamila saw Mina walking with Miranda. It was the first time Mina had spoken to someone else without Jamila at her side. She was making a friend. This was good. Maybe Miranda was telling Mina about her dog Leopold, who only had three legs. Maybe Mina would tell Miranda about Sami.

Jamila saw Alice and Winnie glance over, say something to each other and run off. Minutes ticked by. The shed felt big and empty. Jamila was embarrassed. The colourful posters were up all over the school. She could see three of them from where she stood. She imagined Finn teasing her for trying to start her own choir. She guessed Winnie and Alice were saying it was a bad idea.

Jamila turned her back to the playground, so she didn't have to see all those kids *not* coming to the shed. She took the lid off the box of *klecha* she'd baked and held it out to Eva.

'I made so many,' she said flatly.

'There's still time,' said Eva, taking a biscuit.

Jamila was not so sure, but it was kind of Eva to say so. Just then, Georgia came running over. 'Georgia!' said Jamila.

'Sorry I'm late,' said Georgia, puffing and pushing her glasses up her nose.

'I'm glad you're here,' said Jamila. She

wondered if it was possible to have a choir with just three people. 'It's just us,' she told Georgia, waving an arm around the empty shed.

'So far,' said Eva, standing up. 'What's our first song, Jamila?'

Where would Jamila be without Eva? She would not be in this shed finding a way to keep singing. She would not be starting her own choir or teaching Georgia one of her very own songs. 'It's called, "Change Again",' she said.

Jamila sang. Her voice echoed through the empty space. She hoped Georgia and Eva did not notice the sheet she held was shaking. Singing for just two people seemed harder than singing for a crowd.

Things got better when the girls sang together. They practised the song. Their voices became stronger, and Eva sang a harmony that wove in and out of the chorus. Their voices bounced off the shed walls and out into the playground. Kids started watching. They stopped throwing balls and clambering over monkey bars to listen to the singing.

Marco stood holding the library door ajar. Jamila liked Marco. She felt a strange kind of sadness when he walked away.

Bethany appeared. 'Can I join in?' she asked, when the song came to an end.

'Yes!' said Jamila, handing her a song sheet. She shared a triumphant look with Eva.

Jamila led the song again. Winnie and Alice made their way over. Alice leant against the wall with her arms folded. Winnie picked up a song sheet from the bench. 'Change Again,' she read, when the girls stopped singing. Hearing it now, Jamila thought the title didn't sound so good.

'Did you write that?' asked Alice.

Jamila nodded. Her confidence seemed to be leaking away. Maybe the idea of starting her own choir was ridiculous. She and Eva were just kids.

Jamila wasn't a choir leader. Her songs were childish. Words were spelt wrong. Jamila wished a gust of wind would blow up and whisk away the posters, rip them off trees and walls and make them disappear.

'Yes,' said Jamila. 'I wrote it.'

'So, teach us,' said Winnie.

Jamila heard Mina's laugh and looked out. Mina and Miranda were sitting together. Jamila knew it was good that Mina was making a friend of her own. So why did the sound of Mina and Miranda laughing together make her uncomfortable?

'Hey, Jamila!' said Winnie, clicking her fingers to get Jamila's attention. 'Want to teach us your song?'

Alice looked at her watch. 'Come on, Jamila. Lunch time's nearly over.'

'Okay,' said Jamila. She opened her mouth to sing but stuttered on the first line. Jamila felt everyone's eyes on her. They all waited. The words on the page seemed to blur.

Then Eva began the song. It sounded good. Jamila took a breath and joined in. As she sang, she began to relax. Alice and Winnie soon joined in, too.

While the others ate *klecha* Jamila squeezed Eva's hand. '*Shukraan*,' she said under her breath. Eva knew that meant *thank you*. Eva blinked *you're welcome* with her eyes. Now it *is* a real choir, thought Jamila. She glanced out to the sand pit wall. Mina was sitting alone.

'Mina!' called Jamila. 'Come over!' Mina looked fragile. Now that Miranda was nowhere to be seen, Jamila was back to worrying about her friend.

*13*

Georgia was always reading. She wore purple-rimmed glasses and sipped hot chocolate from a thermos as she turned the pages. She reminded Jamila of Mina's baba, Mohamed. Mohamed read books with thousands of pages and tiny print. He said, 'When you read you can live one hundred different lives without even leaving your chair.'

Georgia asked Jamila if she wanted to join her book club.

'What do you do?' asked Jamila. She was sitting with Mina and Georgia on beanbags in the library.

'We read a book that is so good you can't put it down,' said Georgia. 'Then we meet at my house and talk about it. My dad makes weird muesli bars and I make lemonade.'

Jamila was pleased to be invited to join Georgia's club. She wasn't in the ukulele club or the French club. She didn't play soccer or football.

'I can bring baklava,' said Jamila. 'I make it myself.'

'I love baklava!' said Georgia.

Mina was reading beside Jamila, running her finger slowly along the words.

'Can Mina…maybe…join too?' asked Jamila.

Georgia looked at the book open in front of Mina. It was a picture book with large print. Jamila wanted to tell Georgia that Mina was smart. Really smart. She wished Georgia could see Mina reading in Arabic.

'Do you want to come to book club, Mina?' said Georgia.

Mina held her finger on the page. 'I'm slow,' she said. 'I'm a slow reader.'

'In English,' said Jamila. 'You're not slow reading in Arabic.'

'This is what we're reading this month,' said Georgia. She held up a book. *'Peta and the House Fire.* I've finished it and I keep thinking—what would Peta think? Or what would Peta do now?'

Jamila flipped through the pages.

'I'll need to use the dictionary a lot,' said Mina.

'And ask Mohamed for help,' said Jamila.

'So you'll both come?' asked Georgia.

'I think so,' said Jamila. She looked at Mina.

'Okay,' said Mina. 'I'll try.'

Jamila had never been to Georgia's house or met her dad. She had only been to Eva's and met her Aunt Marisa. Jamila imagined Georgia's house had walls stacked with books. She was curious and a bit nervous. What if Georgia's dad asked questions about life in Iraq or why she left? What should she tell him?

Jamila thought of good things about her country, Eid celebrations and picnicking on the banks of the Tigris River. She pictured the golden mosque and the mountains and lakes. But she also remembered the terrible time she found out Mina's Uncle Mustafa had been shot. And the long days sitting with her cousin in hospital after bomb shrapnel pierced her leg. Images of buildings in piles of rubble came to her mind, and the sound of gunfire coming closer, when there was only a locked door between Jamila's family and the men holding the guns.

Jamila loved her country. In Australia, she felt like a tree whose roots were far away in Iraq. The fighting was a terrible thing and Jamila clung to the hope that one day it would end.

Jamila decided she could tell Georgia's dad her family came to Australia because the people are friendly and the beaches are nice. She had said that before and people nodded like it made sense. As if coming to Australia was a happy choice they had made, instead of a run for their lives.

14

Jamila and Mina were quickly gripped by *Peta and the House Fire* on the bus ride home. Peta, the main character, liked playing with matches. She lit one and then another. Jamila read aloud to Mina. 'With the last match in the box, Peta set fire to an old newspaper and it flickered to life. No one was home. Peta watched as the fire spread to the curtains and flames licked the walls.'

'Oh,' said Mina.

'What is it?' said Jamila.

Mina ran a finger along the bus window ledge.

'I saw a fire,' she said.

'In Iraq?' said Jamila.

Mina nodded. 'I was walking with Baba. A car ahead of us exploded...the ground shook under our feet.'

'A car bomb,' said Jamila. 'They are the worst.'

'A woman was screaming,' said Mina. 'There was so much smoke. There was a man lying on the ground near the car. Baba went to him. He crouched by the man. Then he ran back to me.'

'The man,' said Jamila. 'He was...'

'*Mayit*,' said Mina. Dead. 'We have seen things like this before, Jamila. You know what it was like. But some things just...stay with you.' She looked out the window. 'I remember the orange flames, the black smoke and...this is crazy, but the thing I most remember is the man's white shoes.'

Jamila understood. Unwanted memories stayed with her too.

'I wish I didn't see it,' said Mina.

Jamila paused. 'But you weren't hurt. *Al hamdu li'Allah.*' Praise God. 'And now you are here.'

'I am here,' said Mina.

When Jamila got home, she opened *Peta and the House Fire* and kept reading.

*Peta stood frozen on the spot. The flames were spreading fast. Water, thought Peta. The fire crackled and hissed. Peta ran for a bucket.*

Jamila's shoulders jerked when Mama called her. 'Jamila, come!' Jamila kept reading. She had to know what would happen next.

*Just then, Peta heard footsteps and a key in the front door.*

'Jamila! Can you cook the okra!' called Mama.

'Coming, Mama.'

While Jamila added garlic, lemon juice and tomatoes to the okra and stirred, she wondered what would happen to Peta.

*

Jamila read whenever she could that week. She looked up words like 'extinguish' and 'inhaled' in her dictionary. She read during science. She made notes in her notebook. She couldn't wait for book club at Georgia's. She handed the book to Mina on Friday morning. 'Finished!' she said.

'You've *finished*?' said Eva, eyebrows up.

'It's really good,' said Jamila.

Mina read at recess and Jamila helped her with words she didn't know. They were under the eucalyptus tree with Eva. Jamila saw Eva place her hand against the tree trunk and close her eyes, as if she was listening for a heartbeat. She had been quiet all day.

'Do you want me to ask Georgia if you can join the book club too?' said Jamila.

No,' said Eva. 'Thanks, but…no.'

Eva's forehead was creased with thinking but she didn't say what she was thinking about.

'Are you okay?' asked Jamila.

Eva put her untouched muesli bar back in her pocket. 'I'm not hungry,' she said.

'Mama made *samoon* bread with sesame seeds,' said Jamila, offering some to Eva.

Eva shook her head. 'Not hungry.'

'You're coming to choir at lunch time, aren't you?' asked Jamila.

Eva looked down at her hands.

'Eva?' said Jamila.

Eva nodded. 'I'm coming,' she said, but she didn't look up.

15

Jamila sat with Baba at their kitchen table on a muggy Sunday morning.

'Eva has not been eating, Baba,' said Jamila. 'And Mina and I have book club at Georgia's today, but Eva didn't want to come. Something's wrong.'

'Did you ask her?' said Baba.

'I asked if she was okay,' said Jamila. 'She didn't really answer.'

'You can only listen,' said Baba. 'Ask and then listen. Pay attention.'

Jamila nodded. 'Also, at book club,' she said. 'I don't want Mina to speak Arabic. I mean, not too much. If we speak Arabic...I don't know. Maybe Georgia remembers we are different to her.'

Baba combed his beard with his fingers and squinted like he often did when he was thinking.

'Are we Australian now, Baba?' said Jamila.

'I don't *feel* Australian,' said Baba. 'Iraq is my home. And you, Jamila? Do you feel Australian?'

'I eat Iraqi food and some Australian food. Sometimes Italian food or Vietnamese noodles. I speak Arabic at home and English at school. I listen to Kathem Al Saher, but I also like Australian music.' She threw out her hands. 'I don't know.'

'*Ente* Jamila,' said Baba. The whiskers around his mouth moved with his smile. 'You are Jamila. It is enough.'

Jamila was right about books at Georgia's house. There were two towering shelves in Georgia's bedroom, stacked and stuffed with all kinds of books. Mina and Lan stared.

'I want to be a writer when I grow up,' said Georgia. She wore a t-shirt that said *I'm not quiet, I'm plotting.* 'I won a short story competition,' she added. 'The story prompt was the word *caravan* so I wrote about a boy who ran away from home and lived in a caravan with his dog.'

'You love writing as much as I love singing,' said Jamila.

'I like to draw,' said Mina.

'What about you, Lan?' said Georgia.

Lan shrugged. 'I like playing soccer,' she said. 'And I do gymnastics. I read a lot, too.'

Jamila put her baklava beside Georgia's dad's wonky muesli bars and a jug of Georgia's lemonade.

'Come and sit down,' said Georgia. Jamila sat cross-legged beside Georgia and picked up *Peta and the House Fire.* 'I can understand the way Peta froze when the fire—'

'You mean at the beginning?' said Mina.

'Yes,' said Jamila. She looked at Georgia. 'Peta was in shock, I think. Everything stopped. Her feet were stuck. That happened to me when—'

'Stuck?' said Mina. 'She was stuck?'

'She wasn't *actually* stuck,' said Jamila. 'But she couldn't move…time slowed down.'

'I don't understand,' said Mina.

'You know the feeling of shock,' said Jamila. Mina cocked her head to one side. 'Yes, but—'

'It's okay,' said Jamila. 'It was just a thought.'

Georgia and Lan explained the story to Mina. Each time Jamila tried to talk about the book, Mina slowed her down with questions. She wasn't trying to make trouble. There were words she didn't understand. She couldn't follow the plot. Lan and Georgia were patient with Mina. Jamila sat back and sighed. She tried not to regret inviting Mina to book club.

16

Jamila untied her laces and took off her sneakers. She leant against the banksia's trunk and wriggled her toes. She was wearing her favourite jeans which had a red rose stitched onto the back pocket, and a river-blue headscarf. It was a grey-sky Saturday morning. Mina sat cross-legged nearby drawing the trees and the straight lines of buildings in the distance behind them.

Beside Jamila, Eva took a small photograph from her pocket. Jamila could see the photo was faded and curling at the corners. Eva touched the picture like she was trying to reach through it to the woman who smiled out at her.

'Who's that?' asked Jamila.

'My mum,' said Eva in a small voice. Jamila knew Eva's mum had died when Eva was seven. But Jamila had never seen a picture of her. The woman in the photo had the same smooth skin and green eyes as Eva. She had the same air of calm about her.

'It's nearly her birthday,' said Eva. 'The twenty-second of March.'

Jamila had not forgotten what it had been like to miss Baba when he was still in Iraq. She knew that sometimes it was hard to be around other people when you were busy missing someone. Maybe this was the reason Eva had been so quiet lately. She was missing her mum.

'Last year on Mum's birthday,' said Eva, 'Aunt Marisa took me to the Botanical Gardens. Mum loved gardens.'

Jamila knew that Eva loved gardens too. She often pointed out twisty tree roots or the softness of a petal, or craned her neck to swoon at tall trees.

'After the gardens, we ate chocolate donuts at home,' Eva added flatly, as if chocolate donuts were no better than beans. 'We ate donuts and watched TV.'

Eva didn't have big up and down moods. So it hurt Jamila to feel the fog of sadness coming off Eva. She closed her eyes and imagined she was Eva and felt her grief so much that her throat knotted up.

Eva said, 'Mum would have liked you, Jamila.'

Jamila opened her eyes. She looked closer at the photo. 'She looks like you,' she said. 'You look like her.'

They sat in silence that was sad but not awkward. Then Eva elbowed Jamila gently and Jamila elbowed Eva back. Eva plucked at the grass. 'On her last birthday,' said Eva, 'four years ago, me and Mum and Dad went to the Flower Show.'

Jamila pictured Eva up to her knees in buttercups holding hands with her mum and dad.

'Then the next day,' said Eva, 'Mum went into hospital…and she never came out.'

'Never?' said Jamila. Eva's mum must have died in hospital. Jamila had seen the hospital in Baghdad crammed with moaning, battered people. Hospital would be a terrible place to die.

'How long until…how long was she in the hospital?' she asked.

'Three months,' said Eva. 'She was sleeping a lot. Dad stayed at the hospital, and I was sent home with Aunt Marisa. I wanted Mum to come home. I wanted to stay with her. I thought if she could see me she would get better.' She paused. 'Sometimes I feel angry with her for leaving me.'

Jamila realised that for Eva, the twenty-second of March marked the beginning of her mum dying. It was her last day walking through flowers under the sky with her family.

'We'll be at camp on her birthday,' said Jamila. 'Is that bad?'

'I don't know,' said Eva. 'Maybe.'

Jamila ran a finger along the lines on the palm of her hand, thinking. 'We get pancakes for breakfast at camp,' she said. 'And Georgia said there's a flying fox that zooms so fast it's like flying.'

Eva had collected a small pile of grass. 'I'm not sure I want to be at camp on Mum's birthday,' she said. 'I feel like I'm not supposed to have fun that day. It would feel wrong.' She gathered the grass up in one hand.

'Hmm,' said Jamila. 'Do you want to go to the bridge?' Jamila had learnt that moving your body can sometimes move your thoughts and feelings too. 'Let's sing something.'

Eva opened her hand and let the grass float to the ground. 'Okay,' she said.

Mina was drawing, her head tilted to one side.

'Are you coming?' said Jamila. Mina's drawing book was covered in pencil lines, with shaded areas and space for the sky.

'I want to stay and finish this,' said Mina.

At the bridge with Eva, Jamila sang a song she had written in Arabic and then changed into English. Eva helped her to move words around. They added new ones and took some away, but Eva's attention soon faded. 'I think I'll go home,' she said.

'Do you want us to walk with you?' said Jamila. She glanced at Mina and back to Eva.

'Stay with Mina,' said Eva. 'I'll be okay.' She looked at Jamila. 'Thanks J,' she said. She hugged Jamila with her chin nestled into her shoulder. She smelt like apples.

'Bye Evie,' said Jamila.

17

Mina stood in the middle of Jamila's kitchen with her arms folded that afternoon. 'Show me where everything is,' she said.

'Huh?' said Jamila.

'For cooking,' said Mina. 'I need to know where things are.' She sounded sure of herself. She was telling, not asking.

'Okay,' said Jamila.

Jamila opened cupboard doors and pointed out ingredients and bowls and cake tins.

'Flour,' said Jamila, pointing to the flour.

'Flour,' said Mina, as if making a note in her memory.

'Eggs,' said Jamila, opening the fridge door.

'Eggs,' said Mina.

'Measuring cup.' Jamila started to giggle.

'Measuring cup,' said Mina, giggling too.

Jamila and Mina baked semolina cake. It felt a bit strange without Eva.

'Tell me about Zahra,' said Jamila. 'How was she before you left Iraq?'

Zahra was a girl in Jamila and Mina's class in Baghdad. She had lost sight in one eye after an explosion. She wore an eye patch. Before the explosion, Zahra had a catchy laugh. After the explosion and the surgery that followed, Zahra stopped laughing altogether.

'She stopped coming to school,' said Mina. 'We had a bomb scare and school closed down for three days. When school re-opened, everyone came back except Zahra.'

'Oh no,' said Jamila. 'Poor Zahra. What about Miss Eeda? Was she still at school before you left?'

'Yes. Still there. She asked about you. She was happy you were safe in Australia.'

Jamila missed Miss Eeda. And Zahra. But Mina was here, standing in Jamila's kitchen. Jamila felt a wave of gratitude. She scooped cake mixture onto her pinkie and dabbed it on Mina's nose. Mina gasped. Jamila grinned. Mina stuck a finger into her glass and flicked water at Jamila. Jamila squealed and reached out to tickle Mina's ribs. Mina dashed around the kitchen bench and ran to Jamila's room. Jamila chased her and a pillow fight followed. They took turns pummelling each other and laughing until Mama called for quiet from the next room.

The girls dropped onto the bed and lay panting, with smiles on their faces, letting out small fits of leftover giggles.

18

Eva wasn't at school on Monday. Jamila called her when she got home.

'Hello?' said Eva.

'Hi,' said Jamila. 'It's me.'

'Hi,' said Eva. She sounded down.

'How come you missed school?' said Jamila.

Jamila heard the television in the background at Eva's house and the clanging of pots.

'No good reason,' said Eva. 'I was...tired.' Jamila remembered Eva looking at the photo of her mum at the park.

'Want to come over?' said Jamila. 'I've got an idea for a new cake recipe. Have you got any flour? It's not too late to go to the park and then—'

'No,' Eva interrupted.

'No?'

'No,' said Eva. 'Sorry.'

'Oh,' said Jamila. She felt a little hurt.

'I just don't feel like it,' said Eva.

'It's fine,' said Jamila, but it didn't feel fine.

When they hung up, Jamila sat on the couch.

''Mila,' said Amir, clutching couch pillows as he took wobbly steps towards Jamila.

'Ami,' said Jamila, lifting her little brother onto the couch and touching her nose to his. She took his little hands in hers and pretended to munch on his fingers.

'*Ahbak* Amir,' she said. I love you.


Jamila and Mina whispered to one another in Arabic during class. For Jamila, sometimes speaking her language freely felt like free-falling onto a trampoline that caught you and threw you back up. The feel of the words against her lips and throat reminded her of where she came from and the people she missed.

Mina told Jamila her bedroom in their new flat smelt like rotten fruit and there were finger smudges on the walls. Jamila told Mina she liked Marco. She said she noticed when he wasn't in class but she couldn't look at him when he *was*. When Mina said she already knew about Jamila's crush, Jamila covered her face with her maths book. Mina laughed and nudged Jamila later that day when Marco passed their desk.

As they boarded the bus to go home after school, Jamila saw Miranda with her brother and their dog, Leopold. It reminded her of Mina's dog in Iraq, Sami.

'Tell me about Sami,' said Jamila. 'Who is looking after him now?'

Mina looked out the window and down at her lap.

'What's wrong?' said Jamila.

Mina swallowed. 'I will tell you,' she said. She set her gaze on the back of the seat in front of them. 'One day, Baba took me to the animal shelter after school. It was a cold day. Cold and dark. Sami followed me around while I fed and played with the other dogs. He was wearing the bandana I made for him.'

A tear slipped from a corner of Mina's eye. She swiped it away. 'When I finished my jobs, I sat against the wall with Sami, his chin on my lap.'

'Then what happened?' said Jamila.

'I saw Baba's car,' said Mina. 'I kissed Sami. I ran to the car.'

Mina looked out the bus window. Jamila braced herself for bad news. She felt her neck and shoulders tighten.

'We started driving,' said Mina. 'We drove for,

I don't know, maybe one minute. We heard an explosion.'

Jamila put her hand over her mouth.

'The car shook,' said Mina. 'The bomb was so loud my ears were ringing. Baba's mouth was moving, saying words, but I couldn't hear anything. I looked back. The building was...gone. The animal shelter was a pile of rocks. A cloud of smoke. I called Sami's name. Baba kept driving. I begged him to stop. He said we had to keep going, it wasn't safe. I called for Sami. I kept calling his name,' she said.

Jamila hugged Mina. She remembered Sami and cried for him too.

'I cried for three days,' said Mina. 'On the third day, Baba took me back there.' Mina turned to Jamila. Her cheeks were wet. 'We went to the shelter. It was just rubble. I knew...he couldn't have escaped.'

'Oh, Mina,' said Jamila.

The bus bumped over speed humps and jerked to a halt at the lights.

'I haven't talked about that day with anyone,' said Mina.

'It's terrible,' said Jamila. 'Who could do this?' She felt so angry at the people who had hurt Sami.

'At first, I couldn't believe Sami was gone,' said Mina. 'I didn't want to believe it. Without him, some days I didn't want to live. Some days, I still don't.'

'I'm glad you told me,' said Jamila.

They sat quietly for a moment. Jamila remembered the small blanket Mina kept folded under her pillow. She knew now, without asking, that it was Sami's blanket.

'Do you want to see a drawing?' said Mina, rummaging through her bag. 'Of Sami?'

'Of course,' said Jamila. The drawing Mina took from her school bag was creased and worn, but there he was. Jamila remembered Sami's face, his small pink tongue and the patch of white over one eye. Mina had written in Arabic:

في رعايه الله

In God's hands.

19

When Mina joined Jamila on the school bus the next morning, she said, 'Mama and Baba and I talked about Sami last night. After I told you what happened. We looked at photos of him. Even though it was sad, it was good to remember him in a happy way too.'

'He was perfect,' said Jamila.

Mina nodded. 'Perfect.' She held up a tub. 'I made *makdous.*' Stuffed eggplants. This was the first time Mina had cooked on her own since coming to Australia.

'*Rayie*,' said Jamila. Wow. 'I love your cooking.'

'And I made *halawat sha'riyya*,' said Mina. 'I thought Eva might like to try it.'

Jamila's eyebrows rose up and her mouth watered. She loved the sweet, sticky noodles, golden and chewy, made with rosewater and pistachios.

'Eva will love it,' said Jamila. 'Who wouldn't?'

But Eva was not waiting at the school gates when Jamila and Mina arrived. She was not in the classroom or in the library or playground. Was she still too sad to come to school?

Finn and Winnie were arguing about who was going to go first on the giant swing at camp the following week. Bethany was wearing hiking boots with chunky soles and orange laces.

'I'm practising,' she said, 'for the hike.'

'I hope those boots are snake-proof,' said Finn.

Jamila spun around to face Finn. 'Snakes?' she said.

'Yeah!' said Finn. 'Fat ones, thin ones...' He made a hissing sound and curved his hand from side to side in the air.

'Stop it,' said Jamila, stepping back.

'Mum says you should stamp your feet when you walk,' said Bethany. 'Snakes can't hear, but if you stomp they slither away.' She stamped the floor. 'They can feel it.'

Luna whimpered. Mina went to him. 'It's okay, Luna,' she said. She nuzzled into his fur and calmed him with pats. Jamila wondered if she was thinking of Sami.

'Snakes are more scared of us than we are of them,' said Bethany.

'I don't think they're more scared than Jamila,' said Finn.

'They can *kill* you,' said Beza, bulging her eyes to scare Jamila. 'They're deadly.'

'*You're* deadly,' said Jamila. It was usually better to ignore Beza but the words had slipped out. Jamila *was* scared of snakes. She didn't need Beza to make it worse. Jamila hoped she would not have to share a cabin with Beza at camp.

Jamila was excited about camp. She would need special shoes for hiking and hoped she might find some at the op shop. Mina would need some too. She looked at Beza's ragged slip-on shoes. They looked like they might be okay for the classroom or around the house, but not for climbing a mountain. She didn't say anything. She talked to Mina about jumping on the giant trampoline and going on a nature walk.

'But there are snakes,' said Mina.

'We'll just stomp everywhere we go,' said Jamila. 'Anyway, Finn's just trying to scare us,' she said. 'We won't see one.'

When everyone was at their desks, Miss Sarah put a scrap of paper in front of each student.

Jamila saw dirt under Miss Sarah's fingernails. She imagined her teacher digging small rocks out of Ziggy's hooves.

'Write your name at the top,' said Miss Sarah. 'Then write the names of three friends you would like to share a cabin with.'

Jamila wrote down Mina's name and Mina wrote Jamila's.

'Mina,' said Jamila. 'Eva said she didn't want to come to camp because it is her mum's birthday. What if we put her name down but she doesn't come and then we're put in a cabin with Beza?'

Mina held her pencil against her lips. 'She said she wasn't coming?'

'She didn't think she wanted to,' said Jamila.

Alice and Winnie came over. 'Do you two want to share a cabin with us?' asked Alice.

Jamila looked at Mina.

'You decide,' said Mina.

'Okay,' said Jamila. 'Yes.' She felt a flurry of

excitement.

Underneath Mina's name, Jamila wrote Alice and then Winnie. Mina copied the spelling of their names onto her own piece of paper.

Jamila worried. If Eva did come to camp, who would she be in a cabin with? Miss Sarah was returning to her desk with the lists of names. Jamila considered changing her mind, but then Alice smiled at her and said, 'I'm bringing Tim Tams for a midnight feast. And Winnie's bringing lolly snakes.'

'I will bring *halawat sha'riyya*,' said Mina. 'Sweet noodles.'

Jamila was pleased that Alice and Winnie had chosen her and Mina to share a cabin with them. Miss Sarah slid her desk drawer shut, with the lists of names inside it.

There was no going back now.

20

Eva threaded an arm through Jamila's and dropped her head onto her shoulder. Her hair was damp and Jamila could smell shampoo. All of grade six was gathered by the camp bus. The other grade six teacher, David, helped the bus driver to load bags into the boot of the bus.

Miss Sarah read from a sheet of paper. 'Bethany, Miranda, Poppy and Leo,' she said. 'You will be in cabin number one.'

Jamila had been dreading this moment ever since she had seen Eva at the school gate that morning. Eva *was* coming to camp and Jamila had not put her name down to share a cabin. She wanted to tell her as soon as she saw her. She *planned* to tell her, but there hadn't been a good time.

'Alice, Winnie, Jamila and Mina,' announced Miss Sarah. 'You will be in cabin number two.'

Eva lifted her head off Jamila's shoulder and looked at her. 'But...' she said.

Jamila kept her eyes on Miss Sarah. Her insides jangled.

'Eva, Beza, Lan and Jia,' said Miss Sarah, 'you will be in cabin number three.'

Oh, no. Eva was in with Beza. Jamila stuck her hand up in the air. 'Miss Sarah, can Eva—'

'Nope,' said Miss Sarah, holding up her palm to Jamila. 'We get what we get and we don't get upset.'

Jamila turned to Eva. 'We can still play together,' she said. 'And sit together for lunch and dinner and—'

'I'm sharing a cabin with Beza!' said Eva. She

smacked her hand to her forehead.

Jamila felt bad. She knew Beza could be nasty. And Lan and Jia spoke in Cantonese when they were together. Jamila opened her mouth to confess to Eva that she had not put her name on her list but Alice appeared. She held up a hand for a high-five. Winnie came over too, flushed with excitement. She danced, shaking her hips from side to side. Jamila made a smile shape with her mouth but she still felt bad for Eva.

Jamila told herself it was Eva's fault too. Eva had said she didn't want to be at camp on her mum's birthday. She had left the park early and missed two whole days of school.

Jamila looked around, but Eva was gone. She stood on tiptoes and scanned the crowd. She wove between kids until she found Eva sitting against the fence.

'Want to sit together on the bus to camp?' said Jamila.

'You know I do,' said Eva. 'But you don't have to.'

'I *want* to!' said Jamila. She suddenly wanted to shake Eva and tell her how hard it was having two best friends. 'Oh, whatever,' she said. Her nostrils flared. 'You and Mina can sit together.'

It took three hours to get to Blue River Camp. Eva and Mina sat together and Jamila sat with Georgia across the aisle. Georgia read while Jamila stared out the window.

As the bus drove them away from Melbourne, there were less buildings and more open space. Baba used to drive from Baghdad to Iran, a whole different country, in three hours. Jamila wondered if Australia was the biggest country in the world. She saw cows and sheep and kangaroos out the window.

An hour into the drive, Lan vomited from motion sickness, and then Finn did the same.

Jamila lifted the neck of her top up over her nose to shut out the smell. The bus pulled off the road into a rest area and everyone was shunted off. Jamila looked around. There were picnic tables and toilets and a wall of trees. Mina ran her palm down the trunk of an acacia tree. Jamila remembered wrapping her arms around one side of the wild oak tree in Baghdad while Mina did the same on the other side. They had held hands and pressed their cheeks against the scratchy bark and laughed.

'Can we sit together now?' said Mina.

Jamila looked at Eva, who sat alone at a picnic table. She felt a throb of irritation. She was tired of being caught in the middle. 'I guess so,' she said to Mina.

'*Shukraan*,' said Mina.

'You shouldn't have to thank me,' said Jamila.

Everyone re-boarded the bus and soon they were hurtling along an open freeway. Jamila saw hills and farmhouses. She thought of the drive from her home in Baghdad to her cousin's house. She could picture the lake and the mountains. The colours were different, but the shape of the land rising and falling was the same. Jamila looked forward to the day she would return to Iraq, even just to visit.

21

When the bus finally pulled off the road into a long and bumpy driveway, Miss Sarah stood up the front. 'Here we are,' she said. 'Blue River Camp!'

'There's the giant swing!' Finn shouted, jumping up and pointing. 'I'm first!'

Jamila's stomach did a nervous flip at the sight of the swing. It was dangling at the top of a pole higher than the roof of the camp building.

'And there's the giant trampoline!' cried Alice, pointing in a different direction.

'And an obstacle course!' said Winnie.

Jamila saw a narrow plank strung by chains between wooden poles, two tyre swings, a climbing wall and a flying fox. Did she have to do what they told her? Was camp like school or different? No phone calls. Snakes. A giant swing. Jamila folded her arms over her chest and looked over at Mina. *'Mukhif,'* she said. Scary. Mina gave a vigorous nod.

A woman emerged from the square timber building and introduced herself. 'I'm Karen but you can call me boss.' Thick creases fanned out from her eyes when she smiled and her grey-flecked hair was tied loosely back. 'Now get your gear and follow me.' Her boots were worn and crusted with mud.

Karen helped to unload the bags and then she led the group inside past a rack of pushbikes. She took them into the games room.

'Wow,' whispered Jamila to Mina. She saw a

ping pong table, board games, skipping ropes and racks of sports equipment. Her fear was changing into excitement.

'Epic,' said Finn.

'Cool,' said Winnie.

A tall, thin man appeared. 'Hello,' he said. His long arms hung loose by his sides. He reminded Jamila of her Uncle Yasin.

'I'm Ronan,' he said, blinking slowly. 'Here to help.'

Karen led the group through a dining hall and into a lounge full of beanbags. The lounge was lined with shelves of books. Jamila saw Georgia with her head dropped to one side, reading the titles.

Jamila's cabin had two sets of bunks with thin blue mattresses. Through the window, she saw an open field, hemmed by bush. Jamila imagined snakes and lizards out there. She saw a flock of galahs spiralling up out of the trees. She heard magpies and a bird that sounded like it was laughing.

'That's a kookaburra,' said Winnie. She pointed to a brown and white bird high in a tree. 'Georgia said their beaks grow to ten centimetres long.'

Jamila thought about the Iraqi bulbul chirping its tuneful song. She had seen rosellas, cockatoos and magpies in Australia. She had heard the soft hoot of the tawny frogmouth owl and the tweeting of the butcherbird, but nothing compared to the Iraqi bulbul. She turned to Mina. 'Remember the bulbul?' she said.

'Of course,' said Mina. 'When it sings, you have to stop and listen.'

Jamila rolled out her sleeping bag on a top bunk. Mina lay hers on the bunk underneath. Jamila pictured Eva in her cabin with Beza. She wondered what they were talking about, or if they were talking at all.

When a pop song came over the loudspeaker, they made their way to the dining hall. They found Eva and sat beside her. 'How is your cabin?' asked Jamila. Eva shrugged. Jamila thought of explaining why she hadn't written Eva's name down to share a cabin. But she couldn't bring herself to say the words. She decided she would tell Eva when the time was right.

Jamila's stomach rumbled and she craved Mama's *samoon* bread with lentil soup. Instead, she ate the cheese sandwiches and oranges they were given. She noticed that Eva did not eat much at all.

That afternoon, Jamila took off her shoes and stepped onto the giant trampoline. She sunk down into the rubbery mat. She started with small jumps. She sank deeper into the mat each time and was thrown up higher and higher.

'I'm never getting off!' she called to Mina and Eva.

Mina joined her and soon they were smiling from ear to ear and letting their arms go wide as they jumped. Jamila remembered being on the school swings with Eva before Mina came to Australia, singing together and shouting into the wind.

Eva was standing on the grass and watching. Jamila called to her, 'Come on, Eva!'

She watched Mina, who was so light that when Jamila came down, Mina went up extra high and her arms flew up as she tried to keep her balance. When Jamila turned back to Eva, she saw that she was walking away from the trampoline. The sight of Eva leaving made Jamila sad.

That afternoon, Jamila played ping pong with Mina, Alice and Winnie. Eva sat reading, still and alone.

After dinner, they all spread out on beanbags to watch a movie. Alice and Miss Sarah howled with laughter when the boy in the movie fell into the swimming pool with all his clothes on. Jamila and Mina laughed too, but not Eva. Jamila felt Eva's silence beside her and thought of the song she had been writing:

*My friend, my good, good friend,*
*I see you are sad again*
*I see you are down and blue*
*Where did you go to?*

Alice and Winnie kept chatting after lights-out that night. Jamila wondered if Eva was okay. She hoped Beza was being nice to her. She hoped Lan and Jia were speaking English. She could not shake the image of Eva walking away from the trampoline, and away from her and Mina.

The following morning they all went on a hike up the mountain. There were gum trees with giant roots, and canopies of leaves that shaded the track. There were rocks they had to climb over and fallen trees. Eva walked in front of Jamila with her head tilted forward. She stumbled over tree roots and clung to passing branches to help herself over ditches. There were lizards and birds and there was a laughing kookaburra. Jamila hummed a melody to herself.

Back in her cabin with Mina that afternoon, Jamila sat on her bunk with her notebook and scribbled down song words in Arabic. She did not want to forget them. Jamila knew that when a song comes, you have to catch it. She climbed down from her bunk and asked Mina to help translate the words into good English sentences. Mina helped Jamila write a chorus and a whole new verse.

> *Kookaburra in the tree*
> *Laughing, looking down at me*
> *In the branches up so high*
> *Laughing when you touch the sky*

Jamila and Mina were singing the song together as they walked to the dining hall for lunch. They rounded a corner and bumped into Eva. Jamila stopped singing. Mina did too.

'What's that song?' said Eva.

Jamila paused. 'It's new,' she said.

Jamila and Eva held each other's gaze.

'It's about a kookaburra,' said Jamila. 'You know, the bird that sounds like it's laughing—'

'I know what a kookaburra is,' said Eva. 'It's just...usually you and *me* write songs together.'

Jamila could not remember a time when Eva had been cross with her. But now, Eva's words had a sharp edge.

'You weren't there,' said Jamila.

'That's because I'm in a cabin with Beza,' said Eva, throwing her hands out in front of her. 'Beza! Who squeezed toothpaste onto my soap for a joke! And Lan and Jia, who speak Chinese the whole time! And Beza told me that I *could* have been in a cabin with you, except that you didn't write my name down.' Pink splotches appeared on Eva's neck and rose up to her cheeks as she spoke. 'I told her that couldn't be true. You wouldn't do that, right?'

Jamila felt her heart speed up. 'You were away,' she said. 'And lately, when you *are* at school, it's like you're not actually there. You said you didn't want to come to camp. I didn't know if you were coming. You left the park early and—I don't even know if you want to be my friend.'

'Of course I want to be your friend,' said Eva. 'I thought I was your *best* friend.'

'You're not my best friend,' said Jamila. 'Mina is! I've known her all my life.'

Eva's eyes were wide and shiny with tears. She took one step backwards, and then another. Then she turned and headed back towards the cabins.

Jamila lay on her bunk bed and stared at the

cracks in the ceiling that afternoon. Alice and Winnie played cards on the cabin floor. Jamila wished Alice and Winnie would be quiet so she could think. She had hurt Eva. Why had she said those things? She suddenly missed Amir, his sparkly eyes when he giggled and his warm, dimpled hands holding hers. One more night, she thought. Tomorrow, we go home.

Even though it was afternoon, Jamila fell asleep to the sound of cards slapping onto other cards and Alice and Winnie's chatter. She slept lightly. She dreamt she was at home singing and baking a cake with Eva. She was woken by music coming through the loudspeaker. She realised she had been dreaming.

She was at camp, far from home. And she had fought with Eva.

'That music means dinner,' said Winnie. 'I'm starving.'

'Mmm...I can smell chicken,' said Alice.

'And baked potatoes,' said Winnie.

'Let's go!' said Alice.

As Alice and Winnie wrestled to get out the door first, Jamila climbed down from her bunk. Putting on shoes felt like an effort. Mina came out of the bathroom. *'Enta bekher?'* she said. Are you okay?

'I don't want to see Eva,' said Jamila. 'She's blaming everything on me.'

'Talk to her,' said Mina.

'No!' snapped Jamila. She had a thudding headache. 'I don't feel like being the sorry one. I'm tired of trying.'

22

Jamila sat beside Mina in the dining hall. She jabbed her fork into a piece of carrot and pushed it around on her plate.

'Where's Eva?' asked Winnie, looking at Jamila.

'I don't know,' said Jamila. She brought the carrot up to her mouth, then put it back down.

Alice looked around. 'Maybe she's still in her cabin,' she said. 'Have you seen her here in the hall, Jamila?'

'*No*,' said Jamila.

Mina whispered to Jamila, 'I can't see her anywhere.'

Jamila scanned the faces at the table next to theirs. No Eva. She looked at the table behind them. She stood and roamed her eyes around the room. Finn was kneeling on his chair and talking to Marco with his mouth full. Bethany and Miranda were playing a hand-clapping game. Miss Sarah, David, Karen and Ronan sat at the staff table.

No Eva.

Jamila went over to Lan and Jia. Mina followed.

'Do you know where Eva is?' asked Jamila. Lan and Jia shook their heads.

'She wasn't in the cabin when we came for dinner,' said Jia.

'She wasn't?' said Jamila.

'We have to ask Beza,' said Mina.

Jamila took a breath and crossed the room to Beza. 'Do you know where Eva is?' she asked.

'No,' said Beza. She forked some rice into her

mouth. 'But I heard her crying this afternoon.'

Jamila leaned in to Beza. '*Crying*?' she said. She felt a dip in her stomach.

'I was about to go into our cabin,' said Beza, 'and I could hear her.'

'Did you go in and talk to her?' said Mina. 'What did she say?'

'I left,' said Beza. 'I didn't go in.'

'Why not?' said Jamila.

Beza clinked her fork down onto her plate. 'Look,' she said, 'I'm just not good at that stuff, okay? I'm not good at…saying nice things. Making people feel better.'

Jamila knew that Beza had once teased Eva until a pink rash appeared on Eva's neck and then Beza teased her for the rash. And Lan and Jia were like their own two-person club. They spoke the same language and ate the same food. They shared hair clips and nail polish and they had sleepovers on weekends.

Jamila pictured Eva's face when she had told her she wasn't her best friend. She recalled the shock and sadness in her eyes.

'Do you want me to help look for her?' said Beza.

Jamila brought her fingertips to her forehead. '*Wallah*,' she said. I swear to God. 'You left her alone when she was upset. You've done enough.'

Jamila knew that for Eva, Jamila *was* her best friend. And her best friend had just yelled at her.

Jamila and Mina searched the dining room again and asked Finn and Marco if they had seen Eva. Finn held up a pea and threw it into Marco's open mouth.

'I'm serious,' said Jamila. 'Have you seen her?'

Finn looked at Jamila and Mina. 'Hey, what if a boy walks into your cabin and sees your hair without a scarf on? What happens *then*?'

'What? Nothing,' said Jamila. 'Nothing happens.'

'Boys don't just come into our cabin,' Mina added.

Finn opened his mouth to speak but Marco elbowed him to shush. 'Have you checked the dunnies?' he said. 'For Eva?'

'The what?' said Jamila. Finn laughed and Jamila clenched her jaw.

'The loos,' said Marco. 'Toilets.'

Jamila and Mina walked quickly down the corridor and into the girls' toilets. Jamila had a bad feeling.

'Eva?' said Jamila. Her voice echoed off the tiles. A tap dripped. No answer. 'Eva, are you in here?'

Mina turned off the dripping tap. Jamila crouched to look under the door of every stall.

No shoes. No feet.

'She's not here,' said Mina.

'She has to be *some*where,' said Jamila. Panic was rising inside her. I'll find her, she thought.

I'll find her and I'll say I'm sorry.

'Let's check her cabin,' said Mina.

The corridor was empty. The smell of cooked chicken coming from the dining room made Jamila queasy. She knocked on Eva's cabin door. No answer. They could hear the hum of voices and clicking of cutlery against plates coming from the dining hall. They could hear laughter. Jamila remembered the sound of Eva's laugh. She also remembered Eva's sadness as she held the photo of her mum at the park. She counted days on her fingers. 'Today's the twenty-second of March!' she said.

'And?' said Mina.

'It's Eva's mum's birthday *today*,' said Jamila. 'The twenty-second of March!'

Eva needed a friend today more than ever, and Jamila hadn't even sat next to her in the dining hall.

Jamila knocked harder on Eva's cabin door, a

loud ripple of knocks. She pressed her ear against it. She turned the handle. Inside, sleeping bags and clothes were strewn over bunks. There was a hairbrush on the table under the window. Only one bed was neatly made—Eva's. Jamila recognised Eva's deer blanket laid over her sleeping bag. She could smell Eva's shampoo. She remembered the first time they met outside the Music Room. A lump formed in her throat. She had to find her.

23

Jamila and Mina ran back to the dining hall. They went to Miss Sarah, who was sitting between Karen and Ronan, laughing her gutsy laugh.

'Miss Sarah?' said Jamila.

'Jamila, hi sweetheart,' said Miss Sarah. Her face was still shaped for laughing.

'Eva's not here,' said Jamila. Miss Sarah blinked. 'What do you mean?'

'Not here,' said Mina, stepping closer. 'Not in the dining hall.'

'And not in her cabin,' said Jamila.

'And not in the girls' toilets,' said Mina.

Miss Sarah's smile fell away. She put down her fork and looked around the room. She stood and searched the faces of every child at every table. She cupped her hands to the sides of her mouth. 'Eva Wilson!' she bellowed. Heads turned to her. The hall fell quiet. Miss Sarah repeated Eva's name. Everyone looked around for Eva.

Jamila curled her fingers in, pressing her nails into her palms.

'I'll check the toilets,' said Karen.

'I've already—' Jamila began. But Karen strode past her.

'I'll check the cabins,' said Ronan.

Finn stood and called out Eva's name, the way Miss Sarah had.

Jamila could feel a shift in the air. Was it fear or excitement?

'Bethany!' called Miss Sarah.

Bethany jogged over.

'Go with Jamila and Mina and check the games room,' said Miss Sarah. 'Go straight there. Look in every corner. Then come straight back. Stay together. Got it?'

'We've got it,' said Jamila, grabbing Bethany's hand and pulling her towards the dining room doorway. She heard Miss Sarah making an announcement that boomed through the dining hall. 'Listen up, everyone! I'm calling the roll. I need to hear a clear YES when I call your name, okay?' She sounded frighteningly strict. Not even Finn made a sound.

Jamila's legs felt wooden as they left the hall. She remembered friends not turning up at school in Baghdad. Often, they never returned at all. Everyone worried when a kid was missing from school. Jamila reminded herself this was Australia. Kids didn't just disappear here. There was no fighting. There were no guns. Kids didn't get kidnapped.

Jamila stepped into the games room first, followed closely by Mina and Bethany. There were books and games and balls and beanbags. There was a rubbish bin, a paint box, wooden blocks built into a tower and a basket labelled *Dress Ups*.

No Eva.

'She's not here,' said Bethany.

Jamila opened a door at the back of the room. It was a cupboard holding brooms and mops. She closed it. She put her hand against a window and pushed. The window opened outwards.

'What are you doing?' said Bethany.

'I'm looking!' Jamila snapped. 'What are *you* doing?'

Bethany turned in a slow circle where she stood, running her eyes over everything. 'Jamila,' she said. 'Eva is not in here.'

'Bethany's right,' said Mina. 'She isn't here.'

'No,' sighed Jamila. 'She isn't.' She closed her eyes for a beat. Could Eva be hiding somewhere?

Would she do that?

'We better get back,' said Bethany.

'Yes,' said Jamila. 'Maybe someone's found her. Maybe she's back in the dining room now.'

The class was clustered together in the dining hall when they got back, surrounded by Karen and David on one side, and Ronan on the other. Miss Sarah stood at the front of the group. 'No one is to leave this room,' she announced. Eva had not reappeared. Jamila's heart pulsed. She wished someone would open a window. She could not get enough air.

Was this Jamila's fault? Was Eva missing because of her? Bethany and Winnie were squishing against her sides. Jamila could smell Winnie's chewing-gum breath.

'Jamila!' boomed Miss Sarah.

'Yes?' said Jamila. Her voice was a squeak. Kids moved and space opened up between Jamila and Miss Sarah.

'When did you last see Eva?'

'I...' Jamila stuttered. 'We...' She felt all eyes on her. 'Just before lunch. That's when I last saw her.'

'Where?' said Miss Sarah. She held a clipboard and pen, poised to take notes.

'In the corridor.'

Jamila saw Mina glance at her. Mina had been there when she had argued with Eva. Mina knew. Jamila felt heat rising up from the base of her neck. Her armpits were sweaty.

'What time?' said Miss Sarah. Jamila wanted to talk to Miss Sarah privately. Everyone was listening. 'Um...I don't know. Just before lunch. We were coming to the dining hall—'

'We?' said Miss Sarah. 'You and Eva?'

'No,' said Jamila. 'Me and Mina. We bumped into Eva.'

'So did she come to the dining hall with you at lunch time?'

'No,' said Jamila.

'Jamila and I came together,' said Mina. 'And we didn't see Eva at lunch time.'

'Right,' said Miss Sarah. She looked around the room. 'Who sat with Eva at lunch time?'

Miranda coughed. Outside, a magpie squawked.

Was Jamila the last person to talk to Eva? Were Jamila's cruel words the last thing anyone said to Eva before she disappeared? How long had Eva been missing?

'Has anyone seen Eva since Jamila and Mina last saw her in the corridor just before lunch?' said Miss Sarah, punching out the words. 'Anyone at all?'

Jamila squeezed her eyes shut for a beat and willed someone to speak up. She wanted just one person to say yes, they had seen her. Or yes, they had sat with her. No one did.

Jamila remembered Eva sticking up for Jamila

when kids laughed at her accent. She remembered singing a duet by her side at the school concert. Usually it would be Eva comforting Jamila at a time like this. Had Eva run away because of Jamila? It was not Eva who had been the bad friend. It was Jamila.

'No one leaves this room!' said Miss Sarah. 'Do you understand?'

A murmured 'yes' and nodding heads.

Miss Sarah turned to Karen. 'I'm going to double-check all the cabins,' she said, and left the room.

Everyone waited. The air was thick.

'Not there,' she said, when she returned.

Karen double-checked the girls' bathroom. 'Empty,' she said.

Ronan checked the boys' bathroom and the games room. 'No,' he said. 'Not there.'

Jamila chewed a fingernail. Could Eva be outside in the bush? Had she been bitten by a snake or spider? Or crushed by a falling tree? Had she walked off the campground and been hit by a car? Had she made her way to a train or bus and gone home?

Miss Sarah and Ronan led all the students to the lounge area. 'Stay here for now,' said Miss Sarah. 'Ronan will stay with you.' Ronan nodded. He didn't look worried. Maybe everything would be alright.

'Karen, David and I are going to check the campground,' said Miss Sarah. She turned and spoke in a low voice to Karen and David, pointing in one direction and then another. What was she saying? Where would they look?

Kids watched through the window as Miss Sarah, Karen and David headed outside and split off in different directions to look for Eva. Miss Sarah headed for the obstacle course. David went to the trampoline. Karen made her way towards the giant swing. Jamila wanted to go with them.

She wanted to look for Eva too. How could she stay in this room? How could she stand still at a time like this?

Jamila tried to put herself in Eva's mind, so that she could guess where she might be. Eva was the kind of kid teachers loved. She always put up her hand to speak. She did her classwork. She said please and thank you and handed in homework early. Eva didn't like making trouble or getting too much attention. How could she have gone off on her own?

Jamila thought of the way Eva had changed in recent weeks. She thought about Eva becoming sad and quiet. Jamila had been so busy trying to help Mina and worrying about her own problems that she had not seen that Eva needed her. When she remembered their talk in the corridor, Jamila winced. How could she have spoken to Eva like that?

Jamila looked up at the clock on the wall. The

long hand moved slowly.

*Tick. Tick. Tick.*

Jamila couldn't see Miss Sarah outside any-more. Mina squeezed her hand. *'Min fadlik allah,'* she whispered. Please God. 'Help us find Eva.'

*'Min fadlik allah,'* Jamila repeated.

Through the window, Jamila saw Karen and David making their way along the fence line, looking around and up to the treetops. She heard them calling Eva's name. Jamila wanted to run outside and call Eva's name too.

Soon Miss Sarah returned. She was frowning. There was a smudge of dirt on her arm and leaves in her hair. Eva was not with her. Karen and David returned too, shaking their heads when Miss Sarah looked at them. No. No Eva. Miss Sarah looked around the room until her eyes met Jamila's. She waved Jamila over.

'Yes?' said Jamila.

'Come with me,' said Miss Sarah. Jamila's

heart beat faster. She followed Miss Sarah into the reception area.

'Listen,' said Miss Sarah. 'You're Eva's closest friend. No one knows Eva like you do.' *No one knows Eva like you do.* Jamila felt as see-through as a windowpane. She had let Eva down and maybe Miss Sarah knew it. She wanted to disappear.

'I need you to think,' said Miss Sarah. 'Did she say anything to you? Did she mention anything about running away or...anything that might help us to find her?'

'I...she...' Jamila stammered. 'I don't know where she is.' Jamila burst into tears. 'I don't know.'

Miss Sarah patted Jamila on the shoulder. 'Okay,' she said. 'Okay.'

A car pulled into the driveway and Miss Sarah stood and left the room. Jamila went to the opposite window to see who it was. Mina and other kids joined her.

'Cops!' shouted Finn.

'The police are here?' said Winnie. 'Oh my God.'

'What are the police going to do?' said Alice.

Jamila saw that the daylight was fading. The day was almost over. If Eva was out in that bush somewhere, someone had to find her before dark.

A police officer stepped out of the car. He was a short man with thick shoulders.

'He's got a gun!' said Finn.

Jamila stepped back from the window. She did not trust men with guns.

Ronan had been leaning quietly against the doorframe. Now he came over. 'Hey Finn,' he said. 'And Jamila. Everyone. Let's take it easy, okay? Everything's going to be alright. All of this is just routine. They have to take it seriously when a child goes missing. But I have no doubt we'll find Eva very soon.'

Jamila heard another engine. She saw a second

police car pull into the driveway. This time, a woman in police uniform stepped out. She also wore a gun on her hip. Jamila hoped Ronan would not leave the room. She watched through the window as Miss Sarah and Karen spoke to the police. Two other vehicles pulled into the driveway. 'Who are they?' asked Jamila.

'Volunteers,' said Ronan.

Car doors opened and men and women stepped out of both cars, five of them.

'What are volunteers?' asked Mina.

'Helpers,' said Finn.

Jamila turned to Ronan. 'They're here to look for Eva too?'

'Yes,' said Ronan. 'They're going to search the grounds and the surrounding bushland.'

Jamila watched as the police spoke to the volunteers. Then they all came inside.

A minute later, Miss Sarah stuck her head into the lounge. 'Jamila?' Jamila jerked her head back.

'Yes?'

'You need to come with me,' said Miss Sarah. 'The police want to talk to you. You were the last person to speak to Eva.'

'Okay,' said a voice. *Her* voice. Jamila's mouth was dry. Was she in trouble?

'I was there too,' said Mina, taking Jamila's hand.

'True,' said Miss Sarah. 'Both of you. Come this way. Eva's father and her Aunt Marisa are on their way.'

Oh God. Would Jamila have to tell Eva's family what she had said to Eva? Would they blame her for Eva's disappearance? Would they shout at her? Would they hate her?

Jamila and Mina sat where they were told, opposite the policewoman.

'I'm Sergeant Caley,' said the woman. 'Are you okay?'

Sergeant Caley turned to Miss Sarah, who

was sitting beside Jamila. 'Maybe get them some water? This one looks pale.' She indicated Jamila with a small movement of her hand.

Miss Sarah sat forward. 'You're not in trouble, Jamila. You know that, right? We just need to find Eva.'

Jamila did not know that. She felt like this was all her fault. Miss Sarah brought her water and she sipped. Time had slowed. Word by word, she told the police she had snapped at Eva and told her they were not best friends.

'I wish I could take it back,' she said. 'I shouldn't have said it.'

'*Mutraba*,' said Mina softly, calling Jamila by her nickname. 'They will find her.'

Jamila wondered if she would go to prison for making Eva disappear. Would Miss Sarah call Mama and Baba and say she had done a bad thing? Would Baba look at her with disappointed eyes?

Jamila and Eva were sent back to the lounge

with the other students. They watched the volunteers make their way across the open field and into the bush, searching for Eva. Jamila wanted to search too. She wished she could go back in time, back to seeing Eva in the corridor. She would invite Eva to sit with her to eat lunch.

Minutes ticked slowly by. It was beginning to get dark. Everyone was tense. Police took Ronan, Miss Sarah, Karen and David into the office one at a time.

Jamila couldn't bear doing nothing to find Eva. She turned to Mina. 'Remember when you stood between Sami and the boy holding a stick in the air? In Baghdad? Remember how you saved Sami?'

Mina nodded.

'We can't stand by and do nothing,' said Jamila. 'Eva needs us.'

Mina nodded. 'I am scared for her,' she said.

Jamila lowered her voice. '*Etbaeni.*' Follow me.

24

Jamila could see Ronan was distracted. He was crouched beside a crying boy with grubby knees. Ronan spoke to the boy in a soothing voice. Maybe the boy could feel everybody's worry.

'Now,' whispered Jamila. 'Let's go.' Mina followed Jamila out of the lounge.

'Where are we going?' she asked.

'Back to Eva's cabin,' said Jamila. 'To look for clues.'

Jamila led Mina into Eva's cabin. She picked things up and put them down: books, bags, pillows, hairbrushes. Mina lifted Eva's deer blanket off her bed and shook it out. Then she did the same with the sleeping bag. 'I don't know what I'm looking for,' she said.

'Me neither,' said Jamila. 'Just…keep looking.' She dropped to her knees and looked under Eva's bunk. The floor was covered in dust and there was a spider web in a far corner. Jamila saw a scrunched up piece of paper. 'I see something,' she said.

Mina looked under the bed too. 'I can see a sock,' she said. 'What's a sock going to tell us?'

'Not the sock,' said Jamila. She pointed. 'That,' she said. She ducked her head and slid along the floor on her stomach to get the balled-up paper. She slid back out, brushed dust off her clothes and flattened the paper over her knee. She recognised Eva's handwriting and read the note aloud:

> Today is your birthday. Dad says you have not really gone. You are everywhere. He says you are in the sky and the wind and the trees. Maybe Dad's

just trying to make me feel better. Even if he is, I
like to think it's true. Are you in the trees here too?
Eva.

Beneath the writing Eva had drawn a giant gum tree. Its thick trunk leant over to one side. Fat branches twisted and curled sideways and up. Next to the tree drawing were the words:

Happy Birthday, Mum.

'I know that tree,' said Mina. 'Look!' She pointed out the window. Jamila followed Mina's line of sight. She saw tall trees and short ones. She saw treetops shivering in the wind and birds flitting from tree to tree.

'Over there,' said Mina, stepping closer to the window. 'Leaning over sideways. Look!'

Mina pressed her fingertip against the window. Jamila looked down at the picture and back out at the trees. She squinted. Then she saw it. She saw a tree with its thick trunk bent over like a stretching giant, arms reaching up and out.

'Maybe she's out there,' said Jamila. Her eyes met Mina's.

'Maybe,' said Mina. 'We could show Ronan this note and—'

'No,' said Jamila. 'What if he thinks we're silly? Anyway, I can't bear staying here and doing nothing.'

Mina thought for a moment.

'*Min fathlak*,' said Jamila. Please.

'Okay,' said Mina. 'Then we have to sneak out.'

Jamila felt a surge of excitement. She was finally *doing* something.

'We need a torch,' said Mina.

'Eva brought one,' said Jamila. She rummaged through Eva's bag and pulled out a small torch. She flicked it on.

'Yes!' said Mina.

'Let's go,' said Jamila.

Jamila and Mina snuck down the corridor past

the toilets to the EMERGENCY EXIT door.

'What's emerg...emerge...' stuttered Mina.

'Emergency,' said Jamila. 'You only use an emergency door when there's a big problem and you can't go out the front door. Like right now.' She put her hand on the door handle.

'Right,' said Mina, putting her own hand beside Jamila's. '*Yalla.*'

Outside, Jamila was scared. If they got caught, they would be in serious trouble. The police had seemed nice enough, but would they still be kind if they saw two kids sneaking out of the camp building in the near-dark? And Miss Sarah was a friendly teacher, but Jamila had seen her in a rage when Bethany had stomped her camp boots in the classroom.

Jamila looked to the forest and imagined Eva out there alone. Eva was just as scared of snakes and spiders as Jamila was. She wouldn't venture out into the bush alone unless something was very wrong. If she *was* out there, Jamila had to find her.

Jamila and Mina moved sideways with their backs flat against the wall. They reached the fence that separated the cleared field from the bush and squeezed through the wires. Jamila's heart raced. She stomped her feet to scare snakes away. She breathed slowly in through her nose and out through her mouth. She hummed to calm herself. She held the torchlight on the fence for Mina to squeeze through.

Jamila and Mina stood on the forest side of the fence. They heard rustling and scampering and strange critter squeaks. When they walked, their feet crunched on leaves and twigs snapped against their legs. Jamila held her arm up in front of her face in case she walked into a spider's web.

When they saw beams of light from the volunteers' torches, roaming side to side, they hid behind trees. Then they pushed on through thick scrub. Sticks and rocks stabbed their shins.

Critters rustled through the undergrowth.

'I can't see the tree from here,' said Mina.

'We must be getting close,' said Jamila.

The sky was darkening, a deep blue-black. Jamila sang softly, making up words:

*The dark is only darkness*
*The light is only light*

She remembered singing with Eva and the memory gave her courage.

*It's only in the way I see*
*That I move through the night*

Jamila heard a sound, a soft hum on the last line. She stopped still. 'Did you hear that?'

'No. What?' said Mina.

'Be still,' said Jamila. 'Listen.'

They heard the distant voices of the volunteers. There were squares of light coming through the camp building windows and shadows of movement inside.

'I heard a voice,' said Jamila. She sang again:

*It's only in the way I see*
*That I move through the night*

Jamila heard a voice singing with her. She had sung beside Eva in the school choir so many times that she knew the exact texture of her voice. She recognised it now. 'It's Eva,' she said.

'I heard it too,' said Mina.

Jamila spun in a circle. The light was fading. Trees were silhouettes. She shone her torch around her. She ran the beam up the thick trunk of a gum. The trunk bent over, its branches reaching up and out.

'It's the tree,' said Mina. 'The one in Eva's drawing!'

Jamila's breath caught in her throat when she spied a flash of colour high up in the tree's branches.

'Eva?' Jamila whisper-shouted. 'Is that you?'

25

'I'm here.' Eva's voice.

Jamila's heart turned over. *'Al hamdu li'Allah,'* she said. Praise God. 'Eva. Are you okay? Will you come down?'

Torchlights flashed through the trees. Jamila tried not to think about snakes around her ankles.

'Just leave me,' said Eva.

*'Leave* you?' said Jamila.

'I don't want to go back to camp.'

'Everyone's looking for you,' said Jamila. 'Everyone's worried. Why did you—'

155

'I can't go back,' said Eva.

'The police are here,' said Jamila. 'And your dad and Aunt Marisa. I was so worried. I thought... I didn't know...'

Jamila felt Mina's hand on her wrist. 'We have to go to *her*,' said Mina, pointing to the tree.

'You're right,' said Jamila. She called up to Eva. 'We're coming up!'

Jamila hitched her skirt and reached for the nearest branch, pulling herself up. Bark scratched her shin. Sticks dug into her palms. She found the next branch and pulled herself onto it. A bird squawked and Jamila let out a giggle. She was relieved to be close to Eva again. 'Hello bird,' she said, pulling herself higher. The tree's limbs were strong and held her weight.

When Jamila reached Eva, she swung her legs over to sit on the branch beside her.

Mina climbed up too, holding onto branches to steady herself. Jamila held out her hand to haul

Mina up to sit beside her and Eva.

Eva's face was moon-pale. Mina was puffing from the climb. At last Eva spoke. 'Today is Mum's birthday,' she said.

'I know,' said Jamila. 'When I worked it out I thought—'

'*Astamae*,' said Mina. Listen. Jamila stopped talking.

'The more time passes,' said Eva, 'the further away Mum is from me. I don't like time passing. And what's the point of a birthday when you're not even in the world?'

Jamila didn't know what to say. She thought maybe the point was to remember.

'And you have each other,' said Eva. 'You don't need me anymore, Jamila. You have Mina. You can speak Arabic together. You can talk about the past. It's not your fault, Mina. It's nobody's fault. It's just, when I found out you wrote a song together, and I found out you didn't want to share a cabin with me, it felt like an ending.'

'We didn't know if you were coming to camp,' said Jamila. 'But we should have put your name down. And I shouldn't have said those horrible words to you. I'm sorry. I'm so sorry.'

Now it was Mina's turn to talk. 'I thought I had lost my best friend too,' said Mina. 'Because you two liked doing everything together—singing and cooking. And I felt like I was in the way all the time. I'm not a good singer and I could tell I was making a problem, but I didn't know anyone else.'

'I don't want you to feel bad because of me,' said Eva. 'I never wanted that.'

'The thing is,' said Jamila. She looked at Eva. 'One friend is good, but two is better. I wanted us to be three best friends. I thought it would be easy.' She turned to Mina. 'When you first came Mina, I tried to help you. You were frightened. You needed me. I couldn't be just right for both of you. I kept getting it wrong.'

'No,' said Mina and Eva at the same time. They smiled at one another.

'We can all be friends,' said Mina. 'We can help each other.'

'I think so too,' said Eva.

'I want that more than anything,' said Jamila. 'There's room for three.'

'Oh no,' said Eva. 'Jamila's going to start singing a song. I can tell. I feel like I'm in a musical.'

'*Wallah*, you're right,' said Mina. Eva and Mina laughed together.

Jamila looked up. The sky was clear and speckled with stars. 'Maybe your mum's in the stars, Eva,' she said.

'Maybe,' said Eva.

They looked at the stars and listened to the sounds of the bush in the night.

'We should get back,' said Mina. 'Everyone is worried.'

One at a time, they climbed down from the tree.

Jamila *did* feel like singing. She didn't have to hold the truth inside anymore. As they made their way back to camp, Jamila invited Mina and Eva for a sleepover together at her house.

'I can make dolma for a midnight feast,' she said.

'I will bring *halawat sha'riyya*,' said Mina.

'I will bring popcorn and Tim Tams,' said Eva.

---

Jamila came through the front door of Blue River Camp first. 'She's here!' she called out. Eva came in behind her and stood beside Jamila. Eva's dad rushed over and took Eva into his arms. 'Oh, thank God,' he said.

The policewoman spoke into a radio that was attached to her belt. 'She's here,' she said. Miss Sarah crouched beside Jamila. 'Where was she?' she asked. 'Where have you been?'

Jamila pulled Eva's birthday note from her

pocket and showed it to Miss Sarah. The police came over. Volunteers gathered around too.

'What's this?' said Miss Sarah.

'A clue,' said Jamila. She touched her finger to the tree on the page. 'She was in that tree,' she said. 'We found her there.'

Miss Sarah looked at the police. She looked at the volunteers. She sighed deeply.

'Am I in trouble?' asked Jamila.

Sergeant Caley put a hand on Jamila's shoulder. 'You shouldn't have left the building,' she said. 'You were told not to.' The policewoman looked at Mina and back to Jamila. 'But you have been good friends to Eva.'

'I'm lucky to have them,' said Eva.

'No,' said Jamila. 'We're lucky to have each other.'

'We all are,' said Mina.

Jamila nudged Mina's shoulder with her own. 'We all are,' she agreed.

# Glossary

A list of Arabic words in *Sunflower**

| | |
|---|---|
| *al hamdu li'Allah* | Praise God |
| *'ahbak* | I love you |
| *asif* | sorry |
| *astamae* | listen |
| *biryani* | a rice dish made with spices and minced lamb or chicken |
| *enta bekher?* | are you okay? |
| *ente Jamila* | you are Jamila |
| *etbaeni* | follow me |
| *geymar* | Iraqi clotted cream, served with warm bread and honey or date syrup |
| *habibty* | my love (female) |

| | |
|---|---|
| *ḥalawat sha'riyya* | sweet, sticky noodles |
| *ḥaram* | forbidden |
| *ḥarees* | savoury beef and wheat porridge |
| *ḥasannon* | okay |
| *hummus bi tahina* | hummus with whole chickpeas |
| *klecha* | sweet biscuits made with cardamom |
| *kun hadiana* | be quiet |
| *ladhidh* | delicious |
| *le namshi* | let's walk |
| *makdous* | stuffed eggplants |
| *mayit* | dead |
| *maykhalef* | it's okay |
| *min fadlik allah* | please God |
| *min fathlak* | please |
| *mukhif* | scary |
| *mutraba* | a girl who is always singing |
| *na-em* | yes |
| *rayie* | wow |
| *samoon* | Iraqi flatbread |

| | |
|---|---|
| *showyah* | a bit |
| *shukraan* | thank you |
| *wallah* | I swear to God |
| *yalla* | come on |

*These translations are based on how the words are used in the story. Just as in English, some words would have different meanings in different sentences.

# Acknowledgments

Thank you to the wonderful team at Text Publishing, especially my editor Samantha Forge. Jamila Khodja, Shalini Kunahlan, Kate Lloyd: don't go anywhere! Big thanks to Imogen Stubbs and Amy Grimes for the gorgeous cover.

I am grateful to my Iraqi friend and Arabic translator, Zaid Edward. Thank you also to my agent, Clare Forster. It is so good to have you in my corner.

I am ensconced in a network of supportive and generous writers. Special thanks to this amazing community. I treasure my friends and family above all else. Life is colourless without my people. You know who you are. Thank you.